HITLER SLEPT LATE

AND OTHER BLUNDERS THAT COST HIM THE WAR

JAMES P. DUFFY

PRAEGER

New York
Westport, Connecticut
London

Library of Congress Cataloging-in-Publication Data

Duffy, James P.
    Hitler slept late and other blunders that cost him the war
/ James P. Duffy.
        p.   cm.
    Includes bibliographical references and index.
    ISBN 0-275-93667-8 (alk. paper)
    1. World War, 1939–1945—Germany.   2. Hitler, Adolf, 1889–
1945—Military leadership.   3. Strategy.   I. Title.
    D757.D75   1991
    940.54'0943—dc20   90-25350

British Library Cataloguing in Publication Data is available.

Library of Congress Catalog Card Number: 90-25350
ISBN: 0-275-93667-8

First published in 1991

Praeger Publishers, One Madison Avenue, New York, NY 10010
An imprint of Greenwood Publishing Group, Inc.

Printed in the United States of America

The paper used in this book complies with the
Permanent Paper Standard issued by the National
Information Standards Organization (Z39.48-1984).

10 9 8 7 6 5 4 3 2 1

Copyright acknowledgments will be found at the end of this book.

To Aunt Muriel
(Bubbie)

The loser of this war will be the side that
makes the greatest blunders.

Adolf Hitler

CONTENTS

ACKNOWLEDGMENTS

So many people contributed to the research and writing of this book that it is impossible to mention them all. There are a few who, by their efforts or ideas, were of such help that they should be singled out here.

My close friend Vince Ricci made a major contribution to the entire book and deserves my deepest appreciation. Among the others whose help must be acknowledged are my wife, Kathleen Duffy, whose enthusiastic support is so important; my good friend and adviser Larry Brotmann; and Mary Gallagher, who once again provided a quiet place to work. Finally, there are Alexandra and Olivia; their smiles make the effort worthwhile.

GLOSSARY OF TERMS AND ABBREVIATIONS

OKH   *Oberkommando des Heeres*—High command of the German army

OKK   *Oberkommando des Kriegsmarine*—High command of the German navy

OKL   *Oberkommando des Luftwaffe*—High command of the German air force

OKW   *Oberkommando des Wehrmacht*—Supreme command of all German armed forces

Wehrmacht   German armed forces, including the army, navy, and air force

CAST OF PRINCIPAL CHARACTERS

Field Marshal Walter von Brauchitsch—Commander in chief of the army (OKH) from February 4, 1938, until forced to retire on December 19, 1941, by Hitler, who assumed the post himself. He died in 1948.

Reichsmarshal Hermann Göring—Commander in chief of the Luftwaffe from 1935 until he was removed by Hitler on April 24, 1945. He committed suicide by poison on October 15, 1946, two hours before his scheduled execution.

Colonel-General Franz Halder—Chief of the general staff of the army from September 1, 1938, until he was fired on September 24, 1942. He was arrested by the Gestapo on July 21, 1944, and held in concentration camps until released by Allied forces in 1945. He died in 1972.

Adolf Hitler—Chancellor of Germany from January 30, 1933, until his death by a self-inflicted gunshot to the head on April 30, 1945.

Colonel-General Alfred Jodl—Chief of staff of the armed forces supreme command (OKW) from August 23, 1939, until May 23, 1945. Found guilty of war crimes, he was executed on October 16, 1946.

Field Marshal Wilhelm Keitel—Chief of the armed forces supreme command (OKW) from February 4, 1938, until May 13, 1945. He was found guilty of war crimes and executed on October 15, 1946.

INTRODUCTION

During the 1970s and 1980s several popular novels depicted what the world might have been like had Adolf Hitler succeeded in his military conquests. Among the most popular were Len Deighton's *SS-GB*, Frederic Mullally's *Hitler Has Won*, and Bruce Quarrie's *Hitler: The Victory That Nearly Was*.

The popularity of these and other fictional "what if" accounts of a world that might have been arises from a question that continues to haunt the world even now, almost half a century after his suicide: "How close did Hitler really come to victory?" The answer is "very close," closer than many political and military leaders could bring themselves to admit at the time.

Hitler succeeded in turning a devastated nation into a massive war machine that combined luck, skill, and surprise to roll over most of Europe. Part of his success was based on the weakness and lack of will of many of his enemies.

The popular U.S. view of World War II is that U.S. might and resources won the war against Nazi Germany. Another view holds that long before the United States entered the conflict, Hitler substantially won and then lost the war; his monumental military blunders cost Germany a victory that several times was easily within her grasp. While some historians and biographers have portrayed Hitler as a master military tactician and strategist, others see him as nothing more than "that little Austrian corporal," as Field Marshal Gerd von Rundstedt dubbed him.

Despite spectacular early military successes, Hitler's European conquest ultimately failed largely as a result of two glaring faults in his personal leadership style that caused him to commit disastrous tactical blunders. From a critique of Hitler's military blunders, it can be argued that most, if not all, were tied to one or both of these basic defects in his military leadership.

The first was Hitler's failure to develop a genuine long-range plan, an ultimate goal for his military actions. While he often spoke of *Lebensraum* (living space) that the Greater Germany would wrest from inferior nations in the East, he never formulated a clear plan for utilizing this territory or properly incorporating it into Greater Germany. The only semblance of a serious plan was the idea of seizing territory in swift surprise attacks (blitzkriegs) through the might of his well-organized and superbly led military forces. Actually, what was won through the tactics of "lightning war" was lost by the Nazi Party hacks who were placed in charge of occupied territories. Their cruel actions aroused the animosity of local populations, including many in the East who at first had welcomed German soldiers as saviors.

Blitzkriegs more effectively serve the forces of liberation. The forces of subjugation are better served by a slower, more calculated forward progress that leaves time for an army to consolidate its gains and to neutralize enemy forces that otherwise could continue to operate behind its lines, causing supply and control problems. The wisdom of this strategy was clearly demonstrated by the 1944–45 counteradvance of the Red Army. It pressed slowly forward, permitting Stalin's

Communist Party people to consolidate what had been won by the army and ensure minimum opposition to their control. On the other hand, in Hitler's 1941 invasion of the Soviet Union, fast-striking German forces bypassed and left behind their front lines thousands of Red Army soldiers, many of them in completely intact military units. These soldiers formed the guerrilla forces that wrecked German supply lines throughout the following year.

If the 1941 invasion of the Soviet Union had begun in the early spring, and if the German army had engaged in thorough mopping-up exercises as it moved forward, there would have been little, if any, disruption to the advance of reserve troops or the forward movement of supplies desperately needed at the front.

Hitler's lack of long-range planning was due to his having no real idea of where he was going. Did he want to conquer all Europe? Did he want to include the Indian subcontinent in his empire, or leave that to Japan? Did he want to conquer England or to ally himself with the British Empire? What did he plan to do about the United States once he controlled Europe? These were important questions that should have been addressed long before the war started, but Hitler had no answer for any of them. There is no conclusive evidence that he ever considered many of these vital questions.

In Hitler the absence of a long-range plan was the product of a mind with no vision. In the words of historian Ronald Lewin:

The future was a haze, where he expected remote objectives and imperatives to define themselves only as he drew closer to them. He was incapable of steadily scanning the distant horizon, of working out with careful anticipation the precise circumstances within which he would have to operate when he arrived, and the exact measures which would be necessary to consolidate. The swift and unexpected blow—and then, see what happens.[1]

In the beginning "the swift and unexpected blow—and then see what happens" worked well. This approach was used in the remilitarization of the Rhineland, the rape of Austria, and the conquest of Czechoslovakia. It produced decisive, uncontested victories mainly because the British and French did nothing. With the invasion of Poland the policy faltered and finally collapsed. Hitler failed to recognize that the rules of the game had changed. He maintained the same haphazard approach right up to the end of the war.

A major contributing factor in his failure to develop a concrete plan lay in the way Hitler made his most important decisions. His adjutant, Fritz Wiedemann, explained: "When Hitler was preoccupied with some plans or other, he often shut himself up alone in his room. You could hear him pacing restlessly up and down. He always took the really big decisions . . . alone—mostly against the counsels of his staff and advisers."[2]

The second basic fault in Hitler's military leadership was his conviction that military victories could be achieved largely through the strength of his own will. The triumph of the will was a guiding force in his life. This belief convinced him that the power of his will "had only to be translated into faith down to the youngest private soldier for the correctness of his decisions to be confirmed and the success of his orders ensured."[3] The power of his will could be transformed into victories on the battlefield.

Hitler articulated his belief in the influence of his will when he said, "I live only for the single task of leading this struggle, because I know if there is not a man in there behind it who by his very nature has a will of iron, then the struggle cannot be won . . . ."[4]

On a cold winter day in 1942, Hitler spoke about the impact of his personal willpower. He was discussing the invasion of the Rhineland with a group of Nazis gathered in his East Prussia bunker.

What would have happened on March 13, 1936, if anyone other than myself had been at the head of the Reich? Anyone you care to mention would have lost his nerve. I was obliged to lie, and what saved us was my unshakeable obstinacy and my amazing aplomb.[5]

Hitler's confidence in the power of his individual will led him inevitably to the belief that anything to which he applied his will was made possible by the sheer power of that will. Panzer commander General Heinz Guderian describes Hitler toward the end of the war as clutching the power of his will with "the grim tenacity of a fanatic." It was a willpower that he "deluded himself into imagining would save him and his work from going under."[6]

His unshakable belief in the infallibility of his own will drove Hitler to make the mistake so common to megalomaniacs: He refused to listen to the opinions of those who disagreed with him, even when they were acknowledged experts. This attitude led to what Albert Speer called the "negative selection" of the people around him whose job it was to give him advice and counsel.

Since he regularly responded to opposition by choosing someone more amenable, over the years he assembled around himself a group of associates who more and more surrendered to his arguments and translated them into action more and more unscrupulously.[7]

In the ensuing pages we shall see how Adolf Hitler blundered through the early military victories of the war by means of a combination of extraordinary luck and the weakness, pridefulness, and downright stupidity of his opponents. When that early fortune ran out, Hitler's pathetic lack of genuine military ability surfaced repeatedly as he made grievous decisions that cost Germany men, arms, and eventually the war.

Chapters 2 through 10 examine specific decisions that had

fatal consequences for the Third Reich. Almost half a century later it is still impossible to conclude unequivocally that Germany would have won the war if any one of these decisions had been made differently. Yet these glaring errors of judgment had such great impact on the outcome of the war that the possibility of German victory, had only one mistake not been made, exists.

Individually each of them—for example, allowing the British army to escape from Dunkirk, failing to invade Great Britain immediately after Dunkirk, not recognizing the primary importance of Moscow as a target in the Soviet invasion, and the failure to settle on a single, unified, and coordinated defense policy to deal with the inevitable Allied invasion of northern France—contributed immeasurably to Germany's defeat. Collectively this series of blunders demonstrates the inherent weakness in Hitler's ability as a military planner and leader.

While the German army might have been able to withstand the effects of one or two of these blunders, it could never have survived in the face of so many.

Adolf Hitler's military blunders sealed the fate of Germany and doomed her to defeat, devastation, and a partition that would last for almost half a century.

1

THE MAKING OF A MILITARY GENIUS

But for a few elementary mistakes, he might
have succeeded in conquering the world.
Robert Payne

April 26, 1945, Berlin. The emperor's court is underground.

Above their heads the Third Reich is being pounded into the sandy soil of Berlin. Daytime bombing by the Americans, followed each night by British bomber raids, combine with the heavy guns of the rapidly approaching Red Army to reduce what is left of a once beautiful city into thousands of piles of rubble. The world is taking its revenge on Hitler's Nazi Germany.

Within the past three days the Soviet army has blockaded Berlin and now presses from all sides on the city's meager defenses. The German army chain of command has broken down. Field commanders recognize the futility of following Hitler's orders to attack the superior forces of the Red Army. Intent on surrendering to the Americans or the British, many ignore orders and move their troops west, along with whatever civilians they can rescue from the Soviet advance.

Despite the incessant bombardment, Berlin's defenders, many of them small boys and old men, fight on. They do so because they fear what will happen if they are captured by the Soviets, and because many remain convinced that Hitler's promise of a "miracle weapon" which will save Germany might still become reality.

The leader of the doomed Thousand Year Reich, Adolf Hitler, cowers 20 feet below the city's sewer system. Like a mole, he avoids all sunlight. He shares his cavern home with several dozen people who held positions of power and influence in the nightmare world he had created.

Life in the Führerbunker consists of unending electrically produced artificial days. Darkness comes only when bombs or artillery shells temporarily knock out the generators.

Hitler can feel the death throes of his crumbling empire translated into earth tremors that only yesterday began to cause fatal cracks in the bunker's six-foot-thick walls and to peel away huge chunks of concrete. These walls are his last line of defense against the overwhelming enemy might. That defense is literally collapsing around him.

During the last few days news has reached Hitler that some of his closest colleagues—men who had repeatedly pledged their loyalty to him and his cause, men he had promoted to the highest offices in Germany, men such as Heinrich Himmler and Hermann Göring—had attempted to make deals with the Allies to save their miserable necks. It is some consolation to know they failed.

For Hitler there is no thought of a deal with the enemy and no thought of escape. In his lucid moments, which become increasingly rare as the pressure mounts, the Führer knows there can be no escape. Even if he were successful, escape would make him the most wanted man in history. He knows there can be no sanctuary from his enemies.

Hitler, who has just stripped Göring of all his titles and

honors, sits alone in his study. The room, 10 by 15 feet, is a concrete box devoid of any decoration other than a painting of Frederick the Great. For years that painting has accompanied Hitler wherever he has gone. The room contains a sofa, three upholstered chairs, and a walnut cocktail table piled high with military situation maps that become hopelessly obsolete as quickly as they are prepared. A single ceiling fixture provides barely adequate illumination and contributes to the grim atmosphere.

The Führer sits in a chair at the center of the room. He wears a meticulously tailored brown tweed suit that now hangs loosely on his wasted frame. He tries to control his trembling hands by grasping the arms of his chair so tightly his knuckles turn white. Even his legs have begun to shake. His mind, only occasionally clear and perceptive, is more often murky and confused, as it is now. He is engaged in doing what he has done so frequently during the last few months: placing the blame on others for the failure of his Reich and the destruction of Germany. Now it is the people of Germany who are responsible. It is they who in this hour of mortal danger demonstrate they are unwilling to die with Hitler, and so are unworthy of him. In truth it is Hitler himself who is largely responsible for the chaos, destruction, and death that have descended on Germany.

A careful examination of Hitler's attempt to extend the power and influence of Nazi Germany reveals a man whose military successes depended on the weakness, disunity, or gullibility of his opponents. His failures, which resulted in total defeat, were the product of poor judgment, lack of vision, and an ego that did not permit him to accept competent professional advice when it was most critically needed.

Hitler's rise to power and his acceptance by the German people were the product in part of the "stab in the back" that most Germans felt caused Germany's defeat in World War I. This rationalization allowed Germany to maintain confidence in the power of her military might by shifting the blame for defeat to politicians and others. These included the German Jews, many of whom had remained loyal to the Kaiser throughout the war. It was these forces, so the claim went, that had stabbed the German army in the back and caused the defeat.

The German population had been told, by those with a vested interest in hiding the truth, that the civilian government of imperial Germany had surrendered to the Allies while the army was still capable of winning the war on the battlefields. This notion that the army had been close to victory but had been betrayed by civilian authorities and socialists in the government was a complete fabrication. At a meeting of the Crown Council on October 2, 1918, presided over by Kaiser Wilhelm II, Field Marshal Paul von Hindenburg repeated the demand for an immediate armistice made on September 28 by General Erich Ludendorff, army chief of staff. Ludendorff had called for an armistice "at once." Von Hindenburg told the Kaiser that the army could not hold out another 48 hours. The myth of the "stab in the back" was created by Hindenburg to conceal his role in the armistice. He first used it publicly when testifying before the Committee of Inquiry of the National Assembly on November 18, 1919.[1]

As part of the "stab in the back" armistice, the Treaty of Versailles hung over the German nation like a black cloud. The inequities of the treaty were blamed for the economic collapse of Germany. Every power-seeking politician in the country, including Adolf Hitler, spokesman of the upstart National Socialist German Workers' (Nazi) Party, attacked the treaty.

In many respects the treaty *was* unfair to Germany, which technically was not a defeated nation. She was a signatory to an armistice, not a surrender. Even some of those who had fought against Germany were disturbed by the severity of the treaty. Italian Premier Francesco Nitti called the treaty "a terrible precedent." He decried the fact that German representatives were never heard at the treaty conference, and that they were forced to sign the treaty, against all traditions, when their country was faced with famine and the danger of a violent revolution. He said it was impossible for them to do anything other than sign the treaty.

Articles 42, 43, and 44 of the treaty created a "demilitarized zone" in the Rhineland. This barred any German military facilities or activities in all German territory west of the Rhine River and within 50 kilometers of the river's east bank, an area that included the German cities of Bonn, Cologne, and Düsseldorf. Regaining German territory lost through the signing of the treaty was a desire of the German people that Hitler repeatedly promised to fulfill. His opportunity came in early 1936.

By the end of 1935 Hitler and his Nazi Party were rapidly losing popular appeal. Party registrations had dropped to a trickle and morale surveys conducted by government agencies, including the Gestapo, found strong resentment among the population at the opulent lifestyles of some Nazi officials. Exacerbating the situation was the fact that the standard of living in Germany had plunged dramatically.

While Hitler had concentrated on foreign affairs, he had almost totally ignored domestic policies. The results were growing unemployment, low wages, rising living costs, and severe food shortages even in Berlin, where extra allotments had been assigned. The situation had deteriorated so badly that one report from the Berlin Gestapo described the general standard of living as "extraordinarily miserable." The report also spoke of the potential for violent reaction against the government and the party, and possibly against Hitler himself.

Hitler's reaction to domestic economic and political troubles was not unlike that of many other leaders who have faced the same dilemma throughout history. He opted to raise the banner of nationalism and send troops marching. He decided the time was ripe to break the Treaty of Versailles once and for all and remilitarize the Rhineland. It was also an opportunity to test the tenacity of France and Britain.

In 1936 he sent German troops into the Rhineland to reestablish German military presence there. The German generals expressed fear that the larger and better-equipped French army would repel the German invaders. Hitler ignored their fears and went ahead with his plan.

On March 7 a poorly equipped and undermanned German army marched over half a dozen bridges spanning the Rhine River with banners flying, music blaring, and foreign journalists watching. Without firing a shot they retook this vital territory. During the day the military units crossed the bridges in full view of all interested parties. At night they quietly retraced their steps so they could march over the same bridges the next day, creating the impression of a much larger force than they actually constituted.

Reoccupying the Rhineland was a gamble that could have destroyed Hitler, but did not because of the lack of will of his · opponents, notably the French and British. The Poles, on the other hand, offered to invade Germany from the east if the French would attack the German army and drive it back across the Rhine, a tactic that could easily have crushed Hitler before he got started. Later Hitler described the gamble:

We had no army worth mentioning, at that time it would not even have had the fighting strength to maintain itself against the Poles. If the French had taken any action, we would have been easily defeated; our resistance would have been over in a few days. And what air force we had then was ridiculous. A few Junker 25s from Lufthansa, and not enough bombs for them.[2]

The French and British—or, for that matter, the French alone—had the strength to stop Hitler before he went any farther, but they did nothing of consequence, allowing the Nazi leader to win his first military victory over a larger and more powerful opponent without firing a shot. According to Dr. Earle Ziemke, professor of history at the University of Georgia and consultant to the Time-Life series on World War II, "If the Allies had done something at that time, it probably would have been the end of Hitler."[3]

When the Rhineland invasion proved to be a popular success, Hitler sought other places into which he could extend the Reich and his rule. Two years later, on March 12, 1938, German troops marched into Austria, welcomed by cheering throngs. Hitler himself crossed the German/Austrian frontier at 4 P.M. the same day, standing erect in his Mercedes so the crowds could see him clearly. Hitler was so taken with his reception that he immediately changed his plans for the future of Austria. Instead of having himself elected president of Austria, he decided to form a union of Austria and Germany in the Reich.[4]

The Austrian cabinet agreed, and in early April 48,751,587 adults in both countries, out of 49,279,104 voters, voted affirmatively on the question "Do you accept Adolf Hitler as our Führer, and do you thus accept the reunification of Austria with the German Reich as effected on March 13, 1938?" Czechoslovakia was next.

At the end of World War I, 3.2 million ethnic Germans found themselves part of Czechoslovakia. It was unthinkable to Hitler that these Germans should live beyond the control of the Reich. The region in which they lived was called the Sudetenland. The German minority claimed it was treated shabbily and discriminated against by the Czech population and government. The Sudetenland Germans hated the Prague government, and reunification with Germany was a driving force in their lives.

On September 29, 1938, Great Britain and France ratified the Munich Agreement with Germany and Italy, an accommodation that British Prime Minister Neville Chamberlain assured the world had brought "peace in our time." Czechoslovakia, whose representatives were not allowed to attend the Munich Conference that produced the agreement, was betrayed by the same nations that had recognized her sovereignty as a Western-style republic twenty years earlier. The Sudetenland was taken from Czechoslovakia and annexed by Hitler's Reich.

The following March, Hitler declared that his territorial claims had been satisfied, then promptly proceeded to march in and occupy what was left of Czechoslovakia. The Rhineland, Austria, the Sudetenland, and then the remainder of Czechoslovakia fell to Hitler without the Allies taking any consequential action to stop him. Ironically, the Allies had missed an opportunity to end Hitler's rule, and possibly his life. Except for an elite group in the army high command, few were aware of the first generals' plot against Hitler. The officers had planned a coup to overthrow and possibly execute Hitler, relying on a strong Allied reaction to the invasion of Czechoslovakia and citing the danger of another world war as their motive. Nothing came of the plot because the Allies failed to act.[5]

The first major military blunder for which Hitler would pay the consequences came on September 1, 1939, with the invasion of Poland. The Hitler-Stalin pact, signed earlier that year, divided Poland between Germany and the Soviet Union. Hitler had disdained warnings that the West would not allow him to conquer Poland without provoking a new European war.

To some extent we can understand Hitler's inclination to ignore such warnings. In 1936 he had been told the Allies would drive his army out of the Rhineland. In fact, some of his generals were so convinced the French would attack, they had prepared an evacuation plan designed to save as many German troops as possible in the anticipated debacle. There had also been warnings the Allies would go to war over an invasion of Czechoslovakia. Neither threat materialized.

Poland was the final step. Britain and France had no choice but to declare war on Germany as a result of that invasion. They had publicly committed themselves to the defense of Poland and could not back down from that position, although they engaged in little actual fighting despite their assurances to the Poles. Hitler was stunned by their reaction because he had blinded himself to the facts that made the invasion of Poland different from everything that had come before.

It is ironic that the German invasion of Poland, the act that ignited World War II, was not part of Hitler's early plans for expansion. Along with Hungary, Poland had played a critical role in Hitler's occupation of Czechoslovakia by threatening military action against the Czech rear, a move that helped push the Czechs into surrendering to Hitler. Both Poland and Hungary received Czech territory for their participation.

But a major bone of contention between Germany and Poland had to be settled to Germany's satisfaction before Hitler was willing to accept Poland as a partner in his future plans. The obstacle to that partnership was the fact that Poland had received the largest slice of territory carved from Germany as a result of the World War I armistice.

Through the Treaty of Versailles, Germany had lost the coastal city of Danzig and a 90-mile strip of land leading from the reborn Poland to the Baltic Sea. This unnatural breach, known as the Polish Corridor, cut directly through Germany, separating the main portion of the country from the province of East Prussia. It was as if an internationally enforced treaty gave Canada a 65-mile-wide stretch of land running from Canada's border through Vermont and New Hampshire to the Atlantic Ocean, separating the state of Maine from the rest of the United States. Anyone looking at a pre-1939 map of Europe could not fail to see the potential danger that existed in the partition of Germany by territory ceded to Poland.

In negotiations with the Poles, Hitler demanded that the free city of Danzig be returned to Germany and that Germany be given a secure route through the Polish Corridor that would provide a land link between Germany proper and East Prussia. It was, according to British historian B. H. Liddell Hart, "a remarkably moderate demand in the circumstances."[6] In return, Germany would recognize Poland's right to possession of the corridor and Poland's western borders, which had been established by the Versailles Treaty.

Perhaps overestimating its ability to defend itself against the German army, Poland refused Hitler's demands and sent troops toward Danzig in an unwise display of force. Poland's ambassador to Berlin, Josef Lipski, and Polish Foreign Minister Josef Beck both warned Hitler that his persistence in asking for the return of Danzig would lead to war, thus worsening the situation.

One vast difference between Hitler's threatened invasion of Poland and the annexation of Czechoslovakia was the public assurances given Poland by Britain and France. Had Hitler paid closer attention to what his adversaries were saying and doing, he would have realized that they had no choice but to defend Poland against a German attack.

The salient point was that unlike Czechoslovakia, whose assurances were private, Poland was given public pledges of support. The most important of these was expressed by British Prime Minister Chamberlain in Parliament on March 12, 1939:

In the event of any action which clearly threatened Polish independence and which the Polish Government accordingly considered it vital to resist with their national forces, His Majesty's Government would feel themselves bound at once to lend the Polish Government all support in their power. They have given the Polish Government an assurance to this effect.[7]

But it was not England alone that pledged to support Poland if Germany attacked. Chamberlain said in the same speech: "I may add that the French Government have authorized me to make it plain that they stand in the same position in this matter as do His Majesty's Government."

Despite constant warnings from both the French and the British that they would go to war over Poland, Hitler held firmly to the belief that they would not. Perhaps he had in mind something similar to what Churchill wrote years later in his history of World War II:

Great Britain advances, leading France by the hand, to guarantee the integrity of Poland—of the very Poland which with hyena appetite had only six months before joined in the pillage and destruction of the Czechoslovak State. There was a sense in fighting for Czechoslovakia in 1938, when the German Army could scarcely put half a dozen trained divisions on the Western Front, when the French with nearly sixty or seventy divisions could most certainly have rolled forward across the Rhine or into the Rhur.[8]

So, on September 1, 1939, the German army invaded Poland. Two days later Britain and France declared war on Germany, and World War II began.

The British ultimatum that Germany withdraw from Poland was delivered to the German Foreign Ministry at 9 A.M. by Ambassador Neville Henderson. It gave Hitler two hours to begin the withdrawal or war would exist between the two nations. At 11 A.M. the French ultimatum was delivered. It expired at 5 P.M.

It was now that Hitler revealed both his greatest strength and his greatest weakness. Lieutenant Colonel Nikolaus von Vormann, army liaison officer to Hitler, recorded the former in his notes of that day: "Even today the Führer still believes that the Western powers are only going to stage a phony war, so to speak."[9]

How prophetic that term was, for the period that followed, until the German attack on the West, has become known as the "phony war." Hitler knew full well the weakness of the French mobilization, which would limit the French army to only minor actions for at least ten days. He also knew that the bombing of German cities which the Poles expected the British to start immediately would not materialize. Britain, he suspected, was reluctant to risk the prospect of German retaliation against her own cities.

Deplorably ill-equipped for war, Britain nevertheless launched her first attack on Germany on the evening of September 3. Ten British aircraft flew across the German frontier and dropped 13 tons of leaflets on the Rhur. Printed on the 6 million sheets of paper was the message "Your rulers have condemned you to the massacres, miseries and privations of a war they cannot ever hope to win."

The following day British Blenheim and Wellington bombers, this time armed with bombs instead of leaflets, attacked the German naval facilities at Wilhelmshaven. Five of the 15 Blenheims that made up the first wave of the attack never found the target and returned to England. The remaining ten located Wilhelmshaven. They found the harbor full of German warships totally unprepared for an attack. When the British bombers flew in over the target, the German sailors at first thought they were Luftwaffe planes that had flown off course, so they paid little attention.

When the first British pilot dove out of the clouds to attack the pocket battleship *Admiral von Scheer*, he saw freshly washed uniforms hanging from makeshift clotheslines on the stern of the ship and sailors talking on the deck. He dropped two bombs, but they failed to explode. Two bombs from the next plane also failed to explode. By now the Germans were responding to the attack, and the next plane was shot down. On the second bombing run four Blenheims were shot down by antiaircraft fire from the stationary ships.

By the time the Wellington bombers arrived over the target, the German flak guns were working full-time. Two of the Wellingtons were shot down, and the raid was broken off quickly. Of the 29 bombers that took off from England, 5 failed to find the target and 7 were shot down. The only serious damage done to the German fleet in the harbor was accomplished by a Blenheim that managed to crash into the bow of the cruiser *Emden*, killing a number of sailors. Britain's war against Germany was off to a faltering start.

Many people in Britain, including some members of Parliament, had believed in their government's resolve to aid Poland if the Germans attacked that country. As news of the German destruction of Polish cities from the air reached Britain, a cry for revenge against German cities was raised. Member of Parliament Leo Amery demanded to know of Air Secretary Sir Kingsley Wood why British bombers were not dropping incendiaries on the Black Forest. It was widely known that the dangerously dry forest was being used to house large stores of military supplies, including massive stocks of ammunition.

"Are you aware," the air secretary replied, "that it is private property? Why, you will be asking me to bomb Essen next." The British reluctance to bomb civilian targets or "private property" was based on the hope that the Germans would respond with a similar policy. Had the British taken a realistic look at what the Luftwaffe was doing to "private property" in Poland, they would have realized there was no substance to such reasoning. Kingsley Wood's mention of Essen was a direct reference to the Krupp armament factories located there. It seems the British government entered this war with the misguided notion it could engage in combat only with other combatants, that cities would not be bombed, and civilians would not lose their lives.

On September 7, 8, and 9, French forces crossed the German border at three locations, near Saarbrücken, Saarlouis, and Zweibrücken. They met little resistance. Hitler issued orders to the German army units on the western frontier not to engage the French units unless they were attacked and forced to return fire. He judged his enemy correctly at this point. The French, like the British, were making only a half-hearted effort to relieve Poland. While Hitler hurried to finish off Poland before her allies were forced to come seriously to her aid, the British and French responded as slowly as possible to the German invasion. Everyone except the Poles, it seemed, was playing for time, waiting for the collapse of Poland so additional fighting would be unnecessary.

In the short term Adolf Hitler had judged his enemies correctly. Despite a flurry of activity, the British and French took no effective action against Germany for her invasion and destruction of Poland. His mistake was in believing that the declarations of war by both countries against Germany would simply "evaporate."

Left to their own devices, perhaps the politicians of Britain and France would have managed to ignore their commitment to Poland as they had their commitment to Czechoslovakia. But public opinion in both countries was aroused by the reports of atrocities and murder committed by the Nazis throughout Poland. The politicians were overruled by the people, and a full-blown war was inevitable.

The question that must be asked at this juncture is What would have happened if the French and British had taken decisive action against Germany? In his assessment of the war against Poland, Field Marshal Erich von Manstein offered the opinion that Germany was "bound" to win the war because of its military superiority over the Poles and the surprise with which the campaign was launched. There were two conditions, he said, that had to be fulfilled to assure German victory. The first was German acceptance of an extremely high degree of risk by stripping the western frontier of most troops in order to use the maximum number of military units in the invasion. The second was that the British and French do nothing to take advantage of the skeleton forces that protected Germany's western borders while Poland was being destroyed.

Based on Hitler's correct evaluation of his enemy, Germany's western defenses were left almost nonexistent, but the Allies did nothing of real importance to take advantage of this situation. What would have happened if Britain, and especially France, had struck a real blow at the German frontier? According to von Manstein, "There cannot be any doubt that things might have turned out very differently had the Western Powers taken the offensive in the west at the earliest possible moment."[10]

Although Hitler's decision to attack Poland required that he deplete the German forces manning the western frontier, he readily accepted the risk, gambling that French forces would not attack the German border in strength. The transfer of Hitler's army units eastward left only 11 regular divisions plus the equivalent of a single division of fortress troops defending the western frontier. They were supported by 35 recently formed divisions of second-, third-, and fourth-line troops. These divisions were composed of men who were either raw recruits or at best had been reservists in World War I. In addition, there were no German armored or motorized units facing west; they had all been transferred east.

Even the Luftwaffe had been stripped from the western defenses to support the invasion of Poland. The western arm of the German air force was so weak that several years later Göring's deputy, Field Marshal Erhard Milch, remarked, "If the French campaign had started right after the Polish one, we in the Luftwaffe would probably have been relegated to the sidelines. The war would have been over for us on the fifth day."[11]

Only a thin covering of German forces remained at the frontier, facing a French army of 85 divisions. However, when the French crossed the German frontier, beginning on the night of September 7–8, it was with only a light complement of forces. On September 9 forces in battalion strength from the French Fourth and Fifth Armies moved across the border as the German defense units withdrew.

By September 12 the French army occupied a 15-mile-wide front some five miles inside German territory and had

met no real opposition to its advance. Observers on all sides
could not help wondering what was slowing the French invasion. The French commander in chief, General Maurice
Gamelin, was responsible for France not relieving the pressure on the Poles by attacking the German west with resolve.
Without any indication that German resistance to his advance was strengthening, Gamelin halted his army on September 12 and issued instructions that the French should
prepare for a rapid retreat at the first sign of strong German
opposition.

When the beleaguered Poles protested the lack of French
action they had been promised, Gamelin told them:

More than half our active divisions on the northeast front are engaged in combat. Beyond our frontier the Germans are opposing us
with a vigorous resistance. . . . Prisoners indicate the Germans are
reinforcing their battlefront with large new formations.

Air action from the beginning has been under way in liaison with
ground operations. We know we are holding down before us a considerable part of the German air force.

I have thus gone beyond my promise to take the offensive with
the bulk of my forces by the fifteenth day after mobilization. It has
been impossible for me to do more.[12]

This was a blatant falsehood. In his history of the French
Third Republic, William L. Shirer reported that only 9 of the
85 divisions on the frontier were employed in the "offensive"
and, other than a few reconnaissance flights, there was no
action in the air. There was no "vigorous resistance" and
there were no "large new formations." Not one German soldier, tank, or plane was diverted from Poland to fight against
the so-called French offensive.

Hailed in the French, British, and U.S. press as a victorious
offensive, the French invasion of Germany ended with a
whimper when, on September 30, Gamelin issued orders for
the French army to withdraw during the night. By October 4

all French forces except a light screen of troops had returned across the frontier. These were driven out of Germany by a German counterattack on October 16. By the following night no French troops remained on German soil.

Poland had counted on her allies to open a western front against Germany, forcing the transfer of German forces from Poland. From Britain she received only lip service and two incomplete divisions that were transferred to the Continent too late to be of help. From the French she received even worse: lies about their efforts. Hitler was right: Neither nation had the stomach for a war against Germany. But now they had to mobilize their forces in anticipation of a wider war to come.

The German victory over Poland was credited to several factors. First was the poor leadership of the Polish high command. In the middle of fighting the invaders, several of the best generals were transferred from one battlefront to another in helter-skelter fashion. Finally, in desperation over the high command's mismanagement, two Polish generals, Wladyslaw Anders and Tadevz Kutrzeba, independently disregarded orders from the high command and used their divisions in guerrilla-style war to hit the enemy wherever they thought they could do some good.

The second reason for the victory was the German superiority in leadership, men, and matériel, especially modern weapons such as tanks. Finally, there was the abandonment of Poland by her allies, Britain and France.

Adolf Hitler believed he alone was responsible for the victory. He was so convinced of his military prowess by this and the earlier victories that he decided to take full control of the army himself.

In truth the job of commander in chief of the army had already become "little more than a post box," in the words of General Franz Halder, chief of the general staff.[13] In the weeks following the Polish campaign, Hitler succeeded in accomplishing what Field Marshal von Manstein called "the elimination of the O.K.H., or the General Staff of the Army" from any responsibility for war policy.[14] Hitler now saw himself as a military genius, and his generals as "notorious cowards."

In some perverse way Hitler fancied himself a chess master, moving his armed forces around Europe like so many chess pieces. His assumption of total control over the army was one of his most serious blunders. It gave him the power to make battlefield decisions that went counter to historical precedent and sound advice from others whose knowledge was grounded in experience and training. He regularly referred to his World War I experience as the basis for his decisions, but in truth a corporal stuck in a trench has little understanding of the broader view required of a commander.

Years earlier Hitler's first step toward control of the armed forces, and a major blunder by the German generals, had been the mass swearing of personal allegiance to Hitler by all military personnel on August 2, 1934.

The oath to Hitler was a trade-off by the generals for Hitler's destruction of the *Sturmabteilung* (SA). This quasi-military organization was in constant conflict with the army over which organization was to represent the military arm of the state. Hitler realized that the thugs who composed the SA had outlived their usefulness and that the organized army would suit his future plans for conquest better, so on June 30, 1934, over 2,000 members of the storm trooper organization, including its leader, Ernst Roehm, were killed. The bloody operation, known as the Night of the Long Knives, was carried out primarily by members of the SA's arch rivals, the *Schutzstaffel* (SS).

The generals traded the elimination of the *Sturmabteilung* for an allegiance that would cost them, their army, and their nation dearly. The enormity of the commitment they made to Hitler by taking the oath is described by Robert Payne:

By German tradition there was no escape from such an oath except death. The armed forces were now bound to Hitler by unbreakable

bonds, helplessly at his mercy. They had become his personal instruments to be thrown into whatever adventure he, and he alone,
decided upon.[15]

In this oath lay the seeds of Germany's destruction. With
only rare exceptions the German officer corps was now paralyzed. Their sworn personal loyalty to Hitler forbade them to
disobey orders they knew would result in defeat, and kept
many of them, who might otherwise have joined, out of the
small group of conspirators who plotted Hitler's overthrow
and death. In the end some sought sanctuary in the oath to
disclaim their guilt for the atrocities committed by the German state.

The stage was now set. Hitler saw in himself a master of
military strategy and tactics. His victories in the Rhineland,
Austria, Czechoslovakia, and now Poland confirmed that he,
and not any of his cowardly generals, was the true military
genius. And, most important, he now had full control over
the most powerful of the armed forces, the army. Convinced
that France was not going to make peace, Adolf Hitler now
turned his attention westward.

2

DOOMSDAY ON THE BEACH

Hitler spoilt the chance of victory.
General R. von Thoma

Before attacking the Allied armies gathered in France, Hitler was confronted with the problem of Scandinavian neutrality. While he favored continuation of the neutrality of Sweden, Norway, and Denmark as helpful to Germany, he realized that if he did not end their neutrality, the Allies would. This was especially true for Norway and Denmark. Several factors brought him to this decision.

First was Germany's need for raw materials. Iron ore from Sweden was carried overland by rail to the Norwegian port of Narvik. There it was loaded on German freighters that sailed south in Norwegian territorial waters, protected from Allied attack by Norwegian warships. Had Hitler believed that the Swedish iron ore would continue to enjoy safe passage through Norwegian waters, it is likely he would have delayed or even scrapped any plans for the invasion of Scandinavia.

Among the voices pressing for a German invasion of Norway was that of the Norwegian Nazi leader Vidkun Quisling, who told Hitler during a December 1939 meeting that he had evidence the British planned to occupy Norway's port cities. Quisling asked for Hitler's support for a coup against the Norwegian government.

Although Hitler agreed to help Quisling, he actually took a more wait-and-see attitude toward the planned coup. He was concerned, however, by Quisling's warning about British plans. Hitler knew that Norwegian neutrality was in constant jeopardy from the Allies, who sought a reason to terminate it. In early October his naval commander in chief, Admiral Erich Raeder, had expressed fear that Norway might open its ports to the Royal Navy.

The Soviet attack on Finland in November 1939 gave the Allies a pretext for attempting to send troops into Scandinavia under the guise of aiding Finland. Both Churchill and French Premier Edouard Daladier favored military action against either the Norwegian port of Narvik or the Swedish iron mines at Gallivare. Neither leader made much secret of the fact that he desperately wanted to prevent the iron ore from reaching Germany, even if Norway's neutrality was violated.

Hitler was finally goaded into a decision to occupy Norway by the action of the Royal Navy on February 16, 1940. On that day the captain of the British destroyer *Cossack* carried out a direct order from Churchill to violate Norwegian neutrality, enter Norway's territorial waters, and board the German supply ship *Altamark*. After a short fight in which several German sailors were killed, Captain Philip Vian found 299 British sailors and merchant seamen in the ship's hold. They were prisoners of war being transported from the South Atlantic to Germany.

Norway protested the incursion, but the British rebuffed them. This incident, along with reports of troop movements indicating a planned Allied invasion of Norway, sealed that nation's fate, as well as that of Denmark, which was a stepping-stone to Norway and a link in the communications network between Germany and Norway.

On April 8, 1940, Britain informed Norway that it intended to intercept German ships in Norwegian waters. London failed to reveal to Oslo that it had ordered the Royal Navy to mine Norwegian territorial waters. One day earlier German warships carrying troops for the invasion of Norway had left their Baltic Sea ports and headed north.

Norway and Denmark were simultaneously invaded in the early morning of April 9. Both countries fell within 24 hours. Later that month British and French troops were landed at several Norwegian ports in an attempt to dislodge the Germans, but were driven off.

With his northern borders and supply of Swedish iron ore secure, Hitler returned to his plans for dealing with France and Britain. Despite Germany's rapid success in the conquest of Norway, the big loser was the German navy. While German army losses were minimal, bombardment from Norwegian shore batteries and warships resulted in the sinking of 3 cruisers (including the 10,000-ton armored cruiser *Blucher*), 10 destroyers, and 11 troop transports. A battleship and three more cruisers were damaged so badly they had to be pulled out of service. These were appalling losses for a nation at war with the world's greatest sea power, Great Britain.

On May 10, 1940, German tanks and troops swept across the French, Dutch, and Belgian borders. In a little more than six weeks the French army that had been called the mightiest in Europe was virtually annihilated. The defeat and occupation of France, and of Belgium and Holland, shocked the world, especially the speed with which the Germans accomplished the task.

While it was overlooked by many observers at the time, the German victory was flawed by one of Hitler's major blunders. He allowed the British army to escape capture; it returned to fight another day.

Britain and France had been busy mobilizing for war behind the assumed security of the Maginot Line, a vaunted
system of fortifications that ran from the Swiss border to Belgium. The fortifications had cost France $1 billion and con-
sumed over 26 million cubic feet of cement. In some places
there were concrete structures six levels deep, with miniature
railroads and telephone lines connecting them. All this was
built by a military establishment that sought to protect
France from a German invasion by fighting the trench warfare of World War I over again.

Ironically, when the French signed Hitler's armistice end-
ing hostilities and giving over half of their country to the
Germans, the Maginot Line remained virtually intact. Only
one of its forts had been taken by the Germans. Unable to
penetrate the defenses or convince the French garrison commanders to surrender, the Germans ordered French staff officers to visit each fort and explain to the commanders that
the war was over and that they should surrender. The
Maginot Line had held even after France fell. The Germans
had simply bypassed it.

The offensive in the west was a prime example of Hitler's
true genius, the evaluation of the political will of his enemies
and how that will would affect their military decisions.
France had been in disarray. Her political leadership was divided between those who wanted to fight the Germans and
those who did not. The French military was for the most part
led by old men who were either too tired or lacking in the tal-
ent and ability to defend France that marshals like Ferdinand
Foch and Joseph Joffre had demonstrated in World War I.

Counting the ten divisions of the British Expeditionary
Force (BEF), the Belgian army, and the French army, the invading Germans were outnumbered and outgunned. The
French air force had more modern first-line warplanes available after the German victory than it did when the battle for
France began. Although a plan for massive bombing of advancing German columns had been prepared, most French

planes never saw combat during the weeks between the invasion and the armistice.

Hitler correctly diagnosed the weakness of political will
that paralyzed the French army. His generals, however, saw
only the large, powerful army that would be arrayed against
them, and were concerned that the British would send still
more troops to the Continent. They feared the same fate the
German army had suffered in the last war, when it was hob-
bled by lack of supplies and matériel. They failed to see the
softness of the French heart.

Hitler realized he had to bring France and Britain to the
conference table quickly. He could not keep the Soviet Union
at bay forever. The Nazi-Soviet pact was a stopgap measure
for both sides. He knew Stalin had read *Mein Kampf* and understood its meaning to Russia and her empire. Hitler also
knew from the experience of the previous war that two fronts
spelled doom for Germany. Time was working against him.
He could not afford to wait while his enemies grew stronger.
He hoped to strike fast at the French, forcing a peace settlement on them; then the English, he hoped, would see reason
and come to terms. This had to be accomplished before
Stalin decided to move against Germany.

The original German plan for the conquest of western Europe was devised by Hitler and the general staff, and called
for an invasion spearhead to attack through Holland and
Belgium, then turn south toward France. This was the path
followed by the German invaders in World War I, and everyone, especially the French, expected the Germans to repeat it
in 1940.

Unknown to the French, General von Manstein had convinced Hitler that the main attack should be made through
the Ardennes Forest. Since the French considered the forest
to be impenetrable, especially by armored units, the surprise
would be total. Manstein was correct. Believing the attack on
Belgium and Holland was the main assault, France rushed

the bulk of her army, along with nine of the ten divisions of the BEF, north to counterattack in Belgium.

On May 13 and 14 it became obvious that the strongest German units had pushed through the Ardennes and were advancing along a 50-mile front north of Sedan. The French Ninth Army, attempting to move into a defensive position along this front, was shattered. With their progress virtually unopposed, the Germans smashed across the French countryside. The French high command was thrown into confusion by the German attack through the Ardennes. It ordered the abandonment of the front established in Belgium. The Allied forces were reduced to a withdrawing, defensive war over countryside that was ill suited to such action.

The first German troops reached the Atlantic coast at the port of Abbeville on May 21. France was now cut in two, with a large portion of its army and the BEF, which was actually almost the entire British army, cut off and surrounded. Seven days later the Belgian army surrendered.

The rapid advance of his armies surprised even Hitler. Ensconced in his mountaintop command post not far from the Belgian and Dutch borders, he worked himself into a nervous condition. Terrified of the possibility of military disaster, he berated his generals for the aggressiveness of their campaign. In a diary entry for May 17 General Halder wrote, "The Führer is terribly nervous. He is frightened by his own success, is unwilling to take any risks and is trying to hold us back."[1]

The next day Hitler ordered the protesting generals to slow their advance lest they fall into a French trap. The generals knew there would be no trap because the Allied armies were already in disarray and in retreat almost everywhere, but they obeyed his order. This was the first of Hitler's two personal interventions in the campaign. It was also the first time Hitler had directly involved himself in battlefield decisions. The earlier invasions, including that of Poland, were accomplished by the generals without Hitler's direct participation in battle decisions.

Except for a dispute over the halting of his panzers during which the legendary tank commander General Heinz Guderian resigned in protest, this halt order cost the Germans only two days. Guderian was reinstated by order by General Gerd von Rundstedt, Army Group A commander. (Hitler's second interference, also a halt order, would have devastating long-range effects.)

The Germans continued to close in on the French and British, gradually pushing them into a pocket around the town of Dunkirk, a small port on the English Channel ten miles from the Belgian border. On the morning of May 24 three panzer divisions and two motorized infantry divisions of General Ewald von Kleist's army group were within 15 miles of Dunkirk. Between them and the port were a low-level French infantry division and a much smaller and weaker British infantry force. The general estimated the city and its port could be his in less than one day. At this critical hour the order came to halt all advances against Dunkirk.

As we shall see, there has been, almost from the day the panzers were halted, a dispute about who actually ordered them to stop. Some have placed the blame on von Rundstedt. While the specific order may have been issued by von Rundstedt as field commander, he never would have taken it upon himself to do so without the express approval of Hitler or the army high command.

Earlier that same day Hitler visited von Rundstedt's headquarters and expressed his desire to come to terms with the British. Von Rundstedt told him he wanted to stop the advance temporarily in order to give all units a chance to regroup and prepare for what he saw as the more important task, the turn south and the conquest of the rest of France.

In his history of the war Liddell Hart discussed the meeting between an already jumpy Hitler and the cautious general in these terms:

On the surface it appears to have been unlucky for Hitler that he
chose to visit Rundstedt's headquarters on the morning of the
24th, a crucial moment. For Rundstedt was a wary strategist, careful to take full account of unfavorable factors and avoid erring on
the side of optimism. For that reason he was often a corrective to
Hitler, by providing a coolly balanced estimate—but it did not benefit German chances on this occasion.[2]

Aside from his natural caution, von Rundstedt had little
real experience with or appreciation for the rapid mechanized warfare that was overwhelming the Allied forces on all
fronts. In addition, it is to be expected that he had his mind
on the coming advance south. He had been told by General
Halder that the encirclement of the enemy troops retreating
toward Dunkirk would be handed over to Fedor von Bock's
Army Group B so that he, von Rundstedt, could concentrate
on preparations for the move toward Paris. Dunkirk, Liddell
Hart points out, was barely in "the corner of his eye."

On returning to his mountaintop headquarters, and in face
of opposition from virtually every general, Hitler issued a
stream of orders halting the advance of every unit now moving toward Dunkirk. The retreating French and British armies
were heading toward Dunkirk, from which they hoped to be
resupplied or evacuated. Hitler's actions ensured that they
would be.

The German advance was stopped at the gates of Dunkirk
and the British succeeded in evacuating 365,000 men. Although there were some Czechs, Poles, Belgians, and French
among the troops evacuated, most were British, a fact noted
by the French commanders, whose troops were left to surrender to the Germans.

In typical "stiff upper lip" fashion the British regarded the
retreat from Dunkirk as a triumph. In fact, it was an unmiti-
gated defeat for the British and French armies trapped on the
beaches and harbors of Dunkirk. Winston Churchill turned
Dunkirk into a propaganda victory to prevent the British

people from learning the true extent of the disaster. The BEF abandoned its trucks, tanks, weapons, and allies on the shores of northern France and escaped across the Channel with virtually nothing but the shirts on their backs.

More than 64,000 vehicles and over 500,000 tons of ammunition and supplies were left behind when the defeated forces were evacuated in a human effort of monumental proportions. It was, as British Wing Commander Jeffrey Page recalls, "a victorious retirement. We were beaten, and there was no question."[3]

Dunkirk was both a victory and a defeat for Germany. It was a victory for the German soldiers who swept across France and the Low Countries and cornered the enemy in a small coastal town. It was a lost opportunity with grave repercussions for the future.

As British and French troops streamed into Dunkirk, a strengthening line of defense was built within full view of the panzer troops, who watched in frustration while they were prevented from attacking. At one point Panzer General von Kleist actually disobeyed orders and crossed the Aa Canal, at which he had been ordered to stop. His forces entered the town of Hazelbrouck, cut the British and French lines of retreat from Belgium to Dunkirk, and barely missed capturing the commander of the BEF, General Lord Gort. Von Kleist was told in emphatic terms to return to the opposite side of the canal, which he did.

Three days later the halt order was rescinded and the panzers were given permission to advance. This time the job was not going to be so easy. Tens of thousands of Allied troops had arrived from Belgium to strengthen the town's defenses. Then Hitler interfered again. General von Kleist tells it this way:

It [the resumed advance] had just begun to make headway when it was interrupted by a fresh order from Hitler—that my forces were to be withdrawn, and sent southward for the attack on the line that the remainder of the French army had improvised along the Somme. It was left to the infantry forces which had come down from Belgium to complete the occupation of Dunkirk—after the British had gone.[4]

After Dunkirk the German army headed south to Paris. In front of them the French army stumbled backward until its retreat was turned into a rout that left Paris undefended. On the morning of June 14 the commander of Army Group B, General von Bock, flew into the open city and was standing at the Arc de Triomphe "just in time to take the salute of the first combat troops. It was a parade, not a battle."[5] Two days later the French government requested an armistice and the battle for France was over.

In the first flush of victory over France and the Low Countries, the Germans gave little thought to the consequences of the British escape from Dunkirk. When, in time, it became obvious what a terrible blunder it had been, everyone associated with Dunkirk sought to place the blame elsewhere or to justify the decision.

Looking back some 50 years, it is difficult to disagree with General von Manstein that Dunkirk was a "fatal mistake" for Hitler.[6] Assuming this basic premise is correct, several questions must be asked: Did Hitler personally make the decision to halt the panzer units outside Dunkirk? If so, why? And what would have been the effect on the war if the evacuation from Dunkirk of the BEF had been prevented, and the British force had been captured?

After the war the surviving generals agreed that the order to halt was vigorously opposed by General Halder, who urged Hitler to attack Dunkirk and the retreating British from all sides. Every finger pointed toward Hitler as the chief culprit.

Even von Rundstedt settled the blame squarely on Hitler's shoulders. After the war he told an interrogator:

At that moment [with panzer units less than 20 miles from Dunkirk] a sudden telephone call came from Colonel von Grieffenberg at O.K.H. [Army High Command], saying that Kleist's forces were to halt on the line of the canal. It was the Fuehrer's direct order—and contrary to General Halder's view. I questioned it in a message of protest, but received a curt telegram in reply, saying, "The armored divisions are to remain at medium artillery range from Dunkirk" [a distance of eight or nine miles]. "Permission is only granted for reconnaissance and protective movements."[7]

Some 15 years after the event von Manstein also faulted Hitler: "This successful evacuation must be attributed to the intervention of Hitler, who twice stopped the onward sweep of our armor—once during its advance to the coast and again outside Dunkirk." He later referred to Dunkirk as "one of Hitler's most decisive mistakes."[8]

According to military historian and former British tank officer Kenneth Macksey, the blame for Dunkirk must be shared by both von Rundstedt and Hitler because von Rundstedt's "fears were fed by Hitler."

On the afternoon of the 24th von Rundstedt called the halt, anxious as ever to "close up units to the front", regardless of a steady flow of mechanized forces within reach of the coast—and did so without permission from O.K.H. whose instructions were for Army Group A to be the hammer and Army Group B the anvil to the east of Dunkirk. Not until the evening of the 24th, after von Brauchitsch, the C-in-C, had endured a very unpleasant interview with the Fuehrer, was the halt confirmed on Hitler's authority.[9]

If Macksey's assessment of the chronology of who initiated the halt order is correct, then Hitler is at the least culpable of supporting an error made by von Rundstedt.

Another noted war historian, Edwin P. Hoyt, reverses the chronology: "Hitler had just made his first major tactical blunder of the war. He ordered the halt [outside Dunkirk], backed by von Rundstedt but opposed by von Brauchitsch and Halder."[10]

General Georg von Sodenstein, who served as chief of staff of von Rundstedt's Army Group A, defended his commanding officer's role in the mistake made at Dunkirk by explaining that von Rundstedt "intended to bring the motor to a halt, idling or ticking over, not to stop it."[11]

In a bit of irony, Field Marshal Wilhelm Keitel, chief of the OKW and loyal Hitlerite, attempted to rationalize Hitler's guilt in the Dunkirk decision in his memoirs.

I was present at the vital briefing conference with the War Office when a decision on this question was demanded from Hitler: the fact was that they [army general staff] did not have the guts to accept responsibility for it themselves if, as might happen, the operation failed. However little they were otherwise disposed to depend upon Hitler and accept his advice, in this particular case they unshouldered the burden of responsibility on to him.[12]

General Walter Warlimont, deputy chief of operations for the military supreme command (OKW), believed the idea of holding back the panzers originated with Hitler's two military lackeys, Jodl and Keitel. When he first heard the rumors about the halt, he confronted Jodl, who "confirmed the order had been given, showing himself rather impatient with my inquiries. . . ." Warlimont then discounted any speculation that the initiative came from von Rundstedt, because Jodl "certainly would not have failed to point to Field Marshal von Rundstedt as the one who had initiated or at least supported that order"—and he did not.[13]

The magnitude of the consequences of the German failure to capture the BEF at Dunkirk is reflected in the resolve with which everyone connected with that decision sought to dissociate himself from it after the war. The only major participant unable to do so was Hitler.

Whether Hitler actually issued the order himself or supported von Rundstedt's decision and then expanded it is not the crucial issue. The question of Hitler's precise role in the incident probably never will be completely resolved. What is important is that this was the first time Hitler personally intervened in a campaign, and his interference caused the disaster that was Dunkirk.

It was the beginning of what British author Richard Brett-Smith called "the end of professionalism" in the German army. Brett-Smith described Hitler as "not suited to exercise the highest military command. He was psychologically incapable of delegating authority, and persistently interfered in the chain of command even down to brigade level."[14]

Whatever his role in the restraint of the panzers' progress, it is without question that Hitler made another decision that day which may have contributed even more heavily to the escape of the BEF. He countermanded an order from General Halder, the army chief of staff, without bothering to confer with him.

Halder had ordered that the Fourth Army be detached from von Rundstedt's Army Group A and transferred to von Bock's Army Group B, which was advancing on Dunkirk from Belgium. Disgusted with von Rundstedt's overcautious approach, Halder and General Walter von Brauchitsch, army commander in chief, decided to put the more aggressive von Bock in charge of capturing Dunkirk and the nearly 500,000 enemy soldiers trapped there. After discussing this with von Rundstedt, Hitler rescinded the order and instructed the general to keep the Fourth Army under his command, effectively preventing it from launching an attack on Dunkirk while the British were still vulnerable.

Hitler's order to halt the advance against Dunkirk, or at the least his support of that move, is difficult to explain in rational terms. Several theories have been expounded to account for this incredible blunder. Because of the impact this order had on the subsequent course of the war, each theory deserves careful examination in an attempt to account for Hitler's actions.

One widely supported theory was developed by British historian and tank warfare expert Sir Basil Liddell Hart. He felt Hitler believed that by allowing the BEF to escape, the British government would see the folly of continuing the war and sue for a peaceful settlement. "If the BEF had been captured at Dunkirk, the British might have felt that their honor had suffered a stain which they must wipe out. By letting it escape Hitler hoped to conciliate them."[15]

In reaching this opinion Liddell Hart cites Hitler's attitude at the time he wrote *Mein Kampf*, and again in 1940, that the British Empire was a civilizing and stabilizing force in the world. He was willing to share domination of the world with the British, if only he could get the obstinate little fat man, Winston Churchill, to see it his way. Perhaps this gift of the lives of several hundred thousand British soldiers would do the trick.

At his May 24 meeting with von Rundstedt, Hitler had discussed Great Britain at length, even suggesting that Germany might make troops available to the British government to help put down colonial uprisings.[16]

In his biography of Hitler, Robert Payne suggests it might have been Hitler's respect for the British people that prompted the Dunkirk blunder.

In his confused, elated, and troubled mind many conflicting impulses and ideas were at work. There was his deep-seated respect for the British people learned during his stay in Liverpool during his youth. There was the memory of the British soldiers he had fought against in World War I. There was that "English pride," which in his view was superior to German pride because it derived from the consciousness of an imperial destiny.[17]

Although there is now some doubt about the validity of

Hitler's alleged visit to Liverpool, his respect for the British people was widely known at the time.

Another factor that may have influenced Hitler's decision to stop the army from taking Dunkirk and its enemy troops was the conspiratorial boasting of Air Force Chief Field Marshal Hermann Göring. On May 23, one day before the halt order, Göring telephoned Hitler and told him it would be a political mistake to allow the army generals to achieve this great victory. Many of the generals were suspected of being unfriendly to the Nazi Party, while Göring's air force was a true National Socialist fighting force. The Luftwaffe, he said, would not have its "finest hour." Göring promised Hitler the Luftwaffe would wipe out the enemy troops at Dunkirk. It is ironic that Göring used the same term to describe the expected triumph of his pilots that Churchill used to describe his pilots during the Battle of Britain.

Hitler gave his old friend carte blanche without realizing the Luftwaffe was totally incapable of delivering on Göring's promise. When the chief of the OKW staff, General Jodl, heard of Göring's boast, he said to his adjutant, "There goes Göring, shooting off his big mouth again."[18]

After a "very unpleasant interview" with Hitler on May 24, General Halder recorded the day's momentous decisions in his diary.

The left wing, consisting of armoured and motorized forces, which has no enemy before it, will thus be stopped in its tracks upon direct orders of the Führer. Finishing off the encircled enemy army is to be left to the Luftwaffe![19]

Göring was quick to seize the opportunity to impress Hitler and discredit his old adversaries in the army, apparently without giving any consideration to whether his air force could accomplish the task he so rashly solicited. Field Marshal Albert Kesselring, third in seniority in the Luftwaffe and commander of the Second Air Fleet, which performed so well over France and the Low Countries, described his reaction to Göring's pledge to Hitler in his memoirs.

The Commander in Chief Luftwaffe [Göring] must have been sufficiently aware of the effect of almost three weeks of ceaseless operations on my airmen not to order an operation which could hardly be carried out successfully by fresh forces. I expounded the view very clearly to Göring and told him it could not be done even with the support of VIII Air Group. I pointed out to Göring that the modern Spitfires had recently appeared, making our operations difficult and costly—and in the end it was the Spitfires which enabled the British and French to evacuate across the water.[20]

Göring also overlooked the reality above the battlefields. The Luftwaffe, tired and strained to its limits, was gradually relinquishing control of the air to the Royal Air Force (RAF), a factor that would dramatically affect its ability to destroy the enemy on the Dunkirk beaches. On May 25 the German Fourth Army staff's daily report contained an ominous warning.

For two days now the enemy has had air superiority over von Kleist's [panzer] group and sometimes over Hoth's group. This is something new for us in this campaign, and is caused by the fact that the English have their air bases "on the island itself," and close by, while our units are still for practical purposes really based in Germany.[21]

General Erhard Milch, second in command of the Luftwaffe, attempted to dissuade Göring from his foolhardy venture, pointing out that bombs dropped on the beaches would sink into the sand and explode with little effect. Göring ignored him.

In the end the Luftwaffe failed to perform at Göring's promised level of superiority. The effects of several days of bad weather, combined with the speed and maneuverability of the newly introduced RAF Spitfires, created havoc among the slower-moving German bombers and their fighter escorts. Milch was proved correct about the bombs exploding harmlessly in the sand, and the bomber pilots found the small ships being used for the evacuation difficult targets to hit.

In spite of the reality, Göring bragged to Hitler that his bombers were causing so much destruction in the Dunkirk port that "Only fishing boats are getting through. Let's hope the Tommies can swim."[22]

Later Göring blamed the weather for his failure, but if he had been truthful with himself, he would have admitted that the air force, which he ran like a dilettante instead of a true military leader, was in serious trouble. The air war over Dunkirk was a preview of what the future held for the Luftwaffe. "It was the R.A.F., and not merely some days of bad weather, which refuted his claim" that he could destroy the British forces at Dunkirk.[23] In nine days, 176 German aircraft were shot down over Dunkirk. The British lost 106.

Hitler eventually realized that a great opportunity had been lost at Dunkirk and at various times gave diverse reasons for his actions. When General von Kleist mentioned the lost opportunity to him, he replied, "That may be so. But I did not want to send the tanks into the Flanders marshes—and the British won't come back in this war."[24]

General Halder said that the marshy terrain was one of two reasons Hitler gave him for the halt order. The other had a strange political twist.

This second reason was that for political reasons he did not want the decisive final battle, which inevitably would cause great damage to the population, to take place in territory inhabited by the Flemish people. He had the intention, he said, of making an independent National Socialist region out of the territory inhabited by the German descended Flemish, thereby binding them close to Germany.[25]

Still another reason given by Hitler was that the armored units had suffered heavy losses from enemy fire and mechanical breakdowns, and he needed them all for the drive south toward Paris. No one will ever really know the exact reasons Hitler let the BEF get away. Robert Payne described those reasons as "complex, illogical and very personal."[26]

For the British the successful evacuation of their army became a rallying point as much as if it had been a battlefield victory. A myth grew around the "miracle of Dunkirk" that distorted the truth but served the propaganda purposes of the government of Great Britain.

The consequence to the Germans was that the forces evacuated from Dunkirk became the nucleus of the British army Hitler's troops would have to fight for the next five years. In 1945 von Rundstedt referred to Dunkirk as "one of the great turning points of the war."[27]

In many respects Dunkirk permitted Britain to survive as a fighting nation. There can be no doubt that had the panzer units under von Kleist not been stopped at the Aa Canal, they easily could have smashed through the single British battalion defending the line and taken control of Dunkirk and its harbor and beaches within 24 hours. Almost the entire British army would have been captured.

Adolf Hitler became the unwitting savior of Great Britain, a nation whose predicament "was indeed grim, more dangerous than it had been since the Norman landings nearly a millennium before. It had no army to defend the islands."[28]

The British could hardly have avoided suing for peace had their army been lost in France. Even Winston Churchill, who so masterfully transformed the retreat from the Continent into a victorious achievement, could not have hidden the loss of the more than 200,000 men had they been captured. Britain would have been virtually defenseless that spring and summer without the men who had been rescued.

Without the Dunkirk forces it would have been years before Britain could field an army strong enough to challenge the Axis in Africa or anywhere else. Without the escape from Dunkirk the war would have been over for Britain. Without Great Britain in the war the United States, after the Pearl Harbor attack, would have found it almost impossible to fight a land war against Germany, and there would have been no second front to relieve the pressure on the Soviet Union. While it is true, as Edwin Hoyt wrote, that "The salvation of the army at Dunkirk was the salvation of Britain's war,"[29] it is also true that the salvation of Britain's war was anathema to Germany's war.

For the final word on the price Hitler and the Nazis paid for allowing the BEF to escape from Dunkirk, we turn to Liddell Hart.

His [Hitler's] action preserved the British forces when nothing else could have saved them. By making it possible for them to escape he enabled them to rally England, continue the war, and man the coasts to defy the threat of invasion. Thereby he produced his own ultimate downfall, and Germany's, five years later.[30]

At the same time the British army was being rescued from the north of France, the invading German forces turned south and rushed headlong toward Paris. The French government fled, declaring Paris an open city to prevent its destruction. Within weeks two-thirds of France was German-occupied territory; the remainder of the country was controlled by a French government approved by Hitler, headquartered at the city of Vichy.

What of the fall of France? Was it truly a great victory that redeemed the military genius of Adolf Hitler following the mistakes of Dunkirk, or was France a spineless nation with a large but ineffective army ripe for conquest by the Germans?

When war broke out, France poured more than 400,000 troops into the fortifications of the Maginot Line, where, for the most part, they sat out the war. Then there were the shortsighted, self-serving reactions of many French civilians.

In his history of the fall of France, William L. Shirer describes two scenarios that were repeated many times over.

At one village on the River Indre the local inhabitants extinguished the fuses of explosives already lit by army engineers to blow the bridge there and slow down the German advance. French troops digging in at Poitiers were surprised to see the mayor driving out with a white flag to surrender to the Germans. He was backed by the inhabitants, who had threatened to tear down the barricades erected by the soldiers. French civilians, like so many of the troops, had no more stomach for the fighting that had started only a month before.[31]

   After the war it became fashionable to blame fifth column-ists, or Nazi sympathizers, for treacherous acts that caused the fall of the French Third Republic. The fifth columnists, if they actually existed, were insignificant in number and ac-complishments. However, they made convenient scapegoats to hide the real responsibility for French collapse. In the final analysis, it is clear that the French army and the French gov-ernment were wholly responsible for their own failure. The French leaders were ill prepared for a war they knew was coming. Remember, it was France that had declared war on Germany, not the other way around.

   When the war was over, Frenchmen blamed each other for what had happened in the spring of 1940, even condemning to prison or death men who by their decision to come to terms with the Germans may have saved France from a fate worse than she suffered. For had the Germans occupied all of France, it is clear the French population would have paid a heavier price than it did for France's defeat.

   Guy Chapman, a military writer and authority on French history, describes why France fell so quickly.

There was error everywhere. There was hesitation, there was inde-cision, there was sheer bloody funk at the highest level, among ministers, politicians, generals, civil service chiefs. Among the older officers, there was a shrinking from weapons and methods they did not understand. Worst of all was the general lack of foresight.

Of the French armies of 1870, the Germans said that they were armies made to be beaten. The same preparations were made between 1919 and 1939. Neither politically, nor militarily, nor psychologically was the French nation in a state to face the war into which, against its deepest will, it was inveigled. None the less, its soldiers fought.[32]

3

ENGLAND: TO INVADE OR NOT TO INVADE

The failure to invade England and knock her
out of the war was ultimately fatal to Germany.
Kenneth Macksey

During the early years of his rule Adolf Hitler was never sure
about his feelings toward Great Britain and the British people. At times he would rant about the degeneracy and deca-
dence of the English, and at other times he spoke of his
respect for them and their similarity to the Germans. While
he looked down on most of his opponents, and even his allies, Hitler treated England with a degree of deference that
can be seen in these comments made to a gathering of his
highest-level military officers on May 23, 1939.

The Britisher himself is proud, brave, tough, dogged and a gifted
organizer. He knows how to exploit every new development. He
has the love of adventure and the courage of the Nordic race. . . .
    England is a world power in herself. Constant for three hundred
years. Increased by alliances. This power is not only something

concrete but must also be considered as a psychological force, embracing the entire world.

Add to this immeasurable wealth and the solvency that goes with it and geopolitical security and protection by a strong sea power and courageous air force.[1]

Less than six months later, on November 8, 1939, just one hour before an attempt on his life, Hitler described a completely different England to a meeting of the Old Fighters, the men who took part in his failed 1923 putsch. He spoke to them in a Munich beer hall.

What were the aims of Britain in the last war?

Britain said she was fighting for justice. Britain has been fighting for justice for 300 years. As a reward God gave her 40 million square kilometers of the world and 480 million people to dominate. That is how God rewards the people who fight for freedom; and, be it noted, those who fight for self-determination. For Britain fought this fight as well.

Britain has also been fighting for civilization. Civilization exists in Britain alone—in the British mining districts, in the depressed areas, in Whitechapel, and in the other sloughs of mass misery and destitution.[2]

Hitler's ambivalence toward Great Britain led him to make serious miscalculations and blunders that robbed Germany of potential victories that were easily within her reach. Even after Hitler finally agreed to the invasion of England, having stalled beyond the point of an assured victory, he announced his intentions with vague, unsure language: "I have decided to begin to prepare for, and if necessary to carry out, an invasion of England."[3] If that does not sound like a man uncertain about what he is doing, compare this language with that used to announce other invasions: Poland—"I have decided on a solution by force"; Yugoslavia—". . . must be crushed as speedily as possible"; Russia—"The German Armed Forces must be ready to crush Soviet Russia in a rapid campaign."[4]

Unlike the earlier bold invasions of the countries to Germany's east, as well as of France and the Low Countries, the decision to invade Britain was made too late for success. Moreover, it lacked, at least at the outset, the commitment of Hitler's legendary "unshakable resolve." Hitler was never sufficiently resolute on the question of what to do about Britain. This attitude was directly responsible for Germany's failure to attack England when she lay virtually prostrate and defenseless after the evacuation of Dunkirk.

On the morning of June 5, 1940, Göring's deputy, General Erhard Milch, walked along the water's edge at Dunkirk. The beaches were littered with weapons, shoes, bicycles, motor vehicles, and personal belongings of men sent to war; every sort of military paraphernalia could be found lying in the sand. There were a few bodies, too, but very few, considering the number of combatants who had been trapped there so recently.

As Milch toured the city, its streets and roads clogged with more than 64,000 abandoned vehicles of every description, as well as field guns, machine guns, rifles, and every other sort of weapon strewn about, he realized he was looking at the instruments of Britain's defense. Across the Channel was a nation without the means to defend itself against a concerted attack. Its soldiers had left behind their arms and equipment, the implements that made them soldiers.

Milch rushed back to Göring's special train, parked at a railroad siding near the French border. Since May 16 Göring had been ensconced there, directing the air war. The recent performance of his Luftwaffe had induced a state of continuing euphoria in the overweight field marshal. His planes had attacked more than 60 enemy airfields the first day of the war. They had destroyed large numbers of enemy military aircraft while they were still on the ground. His glider troops had taken the fortresses of Belgium by surprise, and his parachute troops had succeeded in capturing key locations throughout Holland.

Each morning, after attending Göring's war conference, Milch spent six to eight hours flying over the various battle-fields, assessing the situation. Each evening he reported what he had seen to Göring, who passed the information on to Hitler.

Milch's report on the night of June 5 was dramatically dif-ferent from those of previous nights. When the briefing began, Göring was still congratulating himself on the victory. He wanted to know the number of British dead and prison-ers. He was shocked when Milch told him he had seen only 20 or 30 corpses. "The rest of the British Army has got clean away to the other side. They have left their equipment and escaped."[5]

Milch was upset and did not mince words. Had his advice been followed, the German fiasco might have been averted. He acknowledged to Göring that the BEF's being driven from the Continent was a serious blow to the British. "The fact re-mains," he went on, "that they have succeeded in bringing out practically the whole of their army, and that is an achievement which it would be hard to beat."[6]

Deeply disappointed by the news that his desire to give the Luftwaffe its "finest hour" by bombing the British army into oblivion had failed, Göring asked Milch for his recommen-dation. "I would recommend that this very day all our air units—of both the Second and Third Air Forces—should be moved up to the Channel coast, and that Britain should be invaded immediately."[7]

Milch's plan was simple, but as a result of the condition of the British army, it had a great chance of success. Every plane the Luftwaffe could muster would be used either to attack British airfields or as transports to deliver paratroops to key targets in southern England. Their primary mission would be to capture as many airfields as possible, to give the German fighter squadrons bases from which to operate against the rest of the country. Milch told Göring there were several hundred transport aircraft available for immediate use, and with fighter escort they were capable of delivering two or three divisions to Britain on short notice. From these bases German paratroopers could fan out across southern England and head for London, surround the city, and capture the government and the royal family in one sweep. With no army and no central government, Great Britain would collapse.

There was more than a slight gamble in this, but Milch believed what he had seen on the beaches of Dunkirk was strong evidence that the British army was, at that moment, incapable of repelling a determined invasion, even by a small force of several divisions. "If we leave the British in peace for four weeks it will be too late," he told Göring.[8]

Milch of course was correct. Although the British army had escaped, it was an army without weapons. Only a single division remained up to strength and adequately armed for combat. In the words of Sir Basil Liddell Hart, who has been called the greatest military thinker of this century, "If the Germans had landed in England any time during the month after the fall of France there would have been little chance of resisting them."[9]

Another British historian, Ronald Lewin, described the situation in Britain at that time as most susceptible to a German invasion.

Few informed military analysts, and few who, like the author, were serving at the time with the anti-invasion troops along the south coast, would deny that if Hitler had risked all and launched an instant cross-Channel assault immediately after Dunkirk, the likelihood of its failure, though real, would have been small. For what was there to stop it? Virtually every modern tank had been left behind in France and the few remaining in England were obsolete training models. In the whole of the British Army there was only one infantry division whose training, morale and state of equipment justified it as a fighting formation. . . . The field artillery regiment which the author joined on its return from Dunkirk ought to have possessed twenty-four 25-pounder field guns: its total equip-

ment at that moment was one commandeered civilian van! The
pillboxes and antitank traps which had been hastily started had the
appearance of work carried out by some old engineer of the Cri-
mean War.[10]

Anyone watching documentary films of World War II that
show footage of British soldiers and civilian volunteers training with broom handles because they had no real weapons
can understand why Air Chief Marshal Sir Christopher
Foxley Norris arrived at the following opinion.

I'm fairly certain it [a German invasion] would have worked. All
the indications are that it would have worked. It would have been a
pretty puny and unsupported sort of attack, but nothing like as
puny and unsupported as we were. We had nothing at all. I've had
friends who were given the job of defending two miles of coast line
with one World War One artillery piece. We had nothing.[11]

Hitler failed to press the obvious advantage he enjoyed
after defeating the French. Although he appeared well posi-
tioned to defeat the virtually unarmed British army, and to
occupy the whole of England, he was so confident that
Churchill and the British people would end the war that he
actually began the demobilization of the German army. On
July 13, after having told von Brauchitsch that he should prepare for a peacetime army, Hitler ordered the chief of the
army high command to disband 17 divisions and to send another 18 on leave, providing the soldiers could find work at
home.

As absolute ruler of much of Europe, Hitler now controlled
the entire Atlantic coast from northern Norway to the
Franco-Spanish border. France, Belgium, Holland, Luxem-
bourg, Austria, Denmark, Norway, Poland, and Czechoslovakia all answered to Berlin. Britain answered only to her
self-determination.

Winston Churchill spoke to the House of Commons on

June 4. Of Dunkirk he said, "We must be very careful not to assign to this deliverance the attributes of a victory. Wars are not won by evacuations." He ended the speech with a message that should have been loud and clear to Adolf Hitler.

Even though large tracts of Europe and many old and famous states have fallen or may fall into the grip of the Gestapo and all the odious apparatus of Nazi rule, we shall not flag or fail. We shall go on to the end. We shall fight in France, we shall fight in the seas and oceans, we shall fight with growing confidence and growing strength in the air; we shall defend our island, whatever the cost may be. We shall fight on the beaches, we shall fight on the landing-grounds, we shall fight in the fields and in the streets, we shall fight in the hills; we shall never surrender; and even if, which I do not for a moment believe, this island or a large part of it were subjugated and starving, then our Empire beyond the seas, armed and guarded by the British Fleet, would carry on the struggle, until, in God's good time, the New World, with all its power and might, steps forth to the rescue and the liberation of the Old.[12]

The message that Hitler and some of the other German leaders failed to grasp in Churchill's speech was that Britain was not going to capitulate like France. A victory over the British people would be hard and costly. There would be no incidents like those in France. And then there was the problem posed by that largest of all tank traps, the English Channel. There could be no blitzkrieg of massed panzer units against Britain. Invasion would have to be carried out by parachute and glider-borne troops or by landings along the English coast.

A lead player who did not understand the import of what Churchill said was General Jodl, chief of operations for the OKW, who wrote in his diary: "The ultimate German victory of arms over Britain is only a matter of time."[13]

Hitler chose to ignore Churchill's words and continued to hope for some kind of accommodation with the British. He sent peace feelers to Churchill, hoping he would face reality.

He lost precious time waiting for some word from Churchill that the British were prepared to come to terms with the Nazis. Hitler was "incapable of understanding Churchill, who, instead of sending emissaries, openly defied him. That a small island should defy a continent seemed incomprehensible to him."[14]

Hitler's mood during this period can be seen in his handling of the declaration of war against the Allies by Italy. Mussolini had waited until the Germans conquered most of France, then declared war in hopes of sharing in the spoils. The Italians threw 32 divisions against 6 French divisions guarding the Alpine passes. The Italian advance could be measured in feet. The French held their ground.

The original text of the communiqué announcing the Italian entry into the war included the following sentence: "German and Italian soldiers will now march shoulder to shoulder and not rest until Britain and France have been beaten." At first Hitler crossed out "Britain." It was France he wanted beaten, not Britain. Britain might even become an ally against the Soviet Union. He then crossed out the second part of the sentence entirely and rewrote it so now it read: "German and Italian soldiers will now march shoulder to shoulder and will fight on until those in power in Britain and France are prepared to respect the rights of our two peoples to exist."[15]

Hitler continued to vacillate. He rejected one plan after another aimed at Britain, including one to wage bacterial warfare against the island. Weeks slipped by, and still Hitler did nothing. Meanwhile, British industry was working around the clock to replace the RAF fighters that had been lost in the air battles over Dunkirk, and the weapons the army had left on the beaches there.

The only branch of Hitler's armed forces that was working on anything related to an invasion of Britain was the navy. Since November the navy had been doing the kind of preparatory work necessary should an invasion be ordered. This included assembling maps and intelligence relating to the British coastal defenses. It was more of a staff exercise ordered by the commander in chief of the navy, Admiral Raeder, should Hitler suddenly decide to launch an invasion on short notice.

On May 21 Raeder discussed some of the details of a potential invasion plan, but Hitler showed so little interest that the subject was not addressed at their next meeting on June 4. Admiral Raeder brought up the invasion again on June 20, but Hitler failed to respond.

Three days earlier General Warlimont, Jodl's assistant at OKW, recorded that Hitler had not yet expressed interest in invading Britain. "Therefore, even at this time, no preparatory work has been carried out at OKW."[16]

On June 25 the chief of air staff, General Hans Jeschonnek, was asked by the OKW to help prepare its invasion plans. He refused, telling them, "There won't be any invasion, and I have no time to waste on planning one."[17]

As late as July 1, Hitler was still waiting for word that the British were willing to settle. On that day he told the Italian ambassador, Dino Alfieri, that he "could not conceive of anyone in England still seriously believing in victory."[18] The following day, almost a full month since the Dunkirk evacuation, Hitler reluctantly issued an order containing the first tentative steps toward invading Britain.

The Führer and Supreme Commander has decided:
That a landing in England is possible, providing that air superiority can be attained and certain other necessary conditions fulfilled. The date of commencement is still undecided. All preparations to begin immediately.
All preparations must be undertaken on the basis that the invasion is still only a plan, and has not yet been decided upon.[19]

Then Britain delivered a message that Hitler could not fail to understand. On July 3 the Royal Navy attacked the French fleet controlled by the Vichy government, killing more than 1,000 French sailors and sinking the battleship *Bretagne*. The British aim was to prevent the fleet from falling into German hands. Many French saw it as a perfidious act that killed more French sailors in a single day than the Germans had killed since the war started.

This attack, combined with a German discovery in Paris, finally pushed Hitler into approving development of an invasion plan. The Germans had found records from several Allied Supreme War Council meetings in which British representatives explained that the British air staff had a plan to use its newly developed long-range bombers to destroy the Ruhr region, home of more than 60 percent of German industry. Use of air power against the German industrial heartland was to be Britain's strategy, no matter where the German army marched. It was now clear, even to Hitler, that Britain intended to stay in the war.

Nearly a month after the collapse of France, a month of planned reductions of the German army and the anticipation of peace by many Germans, Hitler issued Directive No. 16, "On Preparations for a Landing Operation Against England." The directive began as follows:

Since England, in spite of her hopeless military situation, shows no signs of being ready to come to an understanding, I have decided to prepare a landing operation against England and, if necessary, to carry it out.

The aim of this operation will be to eliminate the English homeland as a base for the prosecution of the war against Germany and, if necessary, to occupy it completely.[20]

Even at this late date Hitler referred to an invasion of Britain being carried out only "if necessary." He continued to harbor hopes that some accommodation would yet be found and to delude himself that Germany and Britain could still somehow have a rapprochement "on the basis of a partition of the world."[21]

Meanwhile, the British government continued to commit all its resources to manufacturing weapons. This effort was supplemented with weapons from the United States. While Hitler wavered, England prepared her defense. Germany's chance for a successful invasion by air or sea slipped farther away with each day's production of weapons and planes.

Planning for the proposed invasion of England, code-named Operation Sea Lion, was done in anything but typical German fashion. Everything was haphazard, with some important individuals either not participating at all or playing only sporadic roles. Hitler absented himself from almost all discussions of the plan except for an occasional meeting with a ranking officer. Göring, whose air force was supposed to play a vital role against Britain, was busy stealing art treasures from museums and private collections throughout the occupied nations. As far as he was concerned, the talk of an invasion of England was a "gigantic bluff" on Hitler's part, an attempt to force the British government to come to terms.[22]

Admiral Raeder, whose navy, along with the air force, was to be the major partner in Operation Sea Lion, had little faith in the whole idea. Milch's invasion plan had relied on the Luftwaffe to strike quickly and without warning, using paratroopers and glider troops. That had been dropped in favor of a plan to land an army in Britain by means of a naval crossing of the Channel. It was doomed to failure before the first invasion ship could set sail. The German navy, which had not yet benefited significantly from Hitler's rearmament programs of the 1930s, had suffered severe setbacks during the conquest of Norway and was in no shape to challenge the Royal Navy for control of the English Channel so that an invasion fleet could cross it. Raeder later claimed that he raised the issue of a waterborne invasion of Britain to "forestall 'irresponsible' suggestions leading to 'impossible demands.'"[23]

Whereas Göring failed to see the weaknesses of his air

force, Raeder saw those of his navy and did his best to postpone serious developments toward an invasion. One thing he did was convince Hitler that a successful invasion of Britain depended on the Luftwaffe gaining undisputed control of the air over the Channel and southern England. He pushed responsibility for taking real action from himself and onto Göring.

During the midsummer of 1940 there was a flurry of activity related to an invasion of Britain. River barges were collected throughout Germany and western Europe, and towed to the Channel and Atlantic ports from which an invasion force might be launched. In Great Britain the possibility of a German invasion was seen as imminent. The Royal Navy was preparing for the defense of the island, as was the Royal Air Force.

For the Germans the activity was just that, activity. The time for an invasion had passed in the first few weeks after Dunkirk, and what was happening now was merely an exercise. Hardly anyone believed it was real.

Hitler, whose indecisiveness on the invasion issue has already been discussed, rapidly lost interest in the subject. His mind was on other conquests. At the Obersalzberg on July 21 he told a meeting of his military commanders that he was determined to launch an invasion of the Soviet Union. Hitler also had been contemplating sending several divisions through Spain to capture Gibraltar from the rear. This plan, which included the occupation of Portugal, came to nothing when, later in the year, General Franco refused the Germans permission to enter Spain.

The most important flaw in the invasion of England was the absence of a long-range plan. Hitler had given no thought to dealing with a hostile Britain after the conquest of Holland, Belgium, and France. He was so convinced that a victory on the Continent would bring Britain to the bargaining table that he saw time spent on planning action against the British Isles as wasted. Germany's failure to deal successfully with a recalcitrant Great Britain was a direct result of Hitler's failure to accept the importance of long-range planning. It was an example of his attitude summed up in the description "The swift and unexpected blow—and then, see what happens."

If Germany had prepared for victory in France and a quick blow at the British, the war would have taken an entirely different turn, and perhaps would have ended when German troops marched through London as they had marched through Paris.

Until Milch and other military commanders looked at the debris in Dunkirk and then across the Channel, no one had given serious thought to such a campaign. It appears that Admiral Raeder was the only high-ranking officer to have given any consideration to the idea, and most of the "planning" activity by his navy was done to ward off anyone else's idea that Germany's puny navy could protect an invasion force from the Royal Navy. It had been a long time—not since the early years of World War I—that Germany had thought of herself as a naval power.

It would have been difficult to find someone among the high-ranking German officers who really believed a naval landing invasion of England was going to take place. Nevertheless, the preparations went on, doing great damage to the German economy, since virtually every river barge in German-controlled Europe was transported to the coast and fitted to carry men and arms across the Channel. Construction of U-boats and the battleship *Tirpitz* was hampered so that landing barges, of which Germany possessed none, could be built. No one in Germany had any experience in planning and executing a naval landing, and hardly anyone expected such a landing was going to take place.

Hitler himself had acknowledged as much when he said to his naval adjutant, Captain Karl Jesko von Puttkamer, "How can we do an operation of this sort? It looks completely impossible to me. Losses would be heavy and [there would be] no guarantee of success."[24]

The attitude of the naval officers directly involved in Operation Sea Lion was expressed by Lieutenant Commander Heinrich Bartels, who was responsible for the invasion preparations in and around Dunkirk. When Admiral Raeder asked him, "Tell me your opinion, do you think we shall make it across to England?" Bartels's answer was honest and forthright: ". . . the thing will be a flop from the start."[25]

Although a landing on the English beaches had been reduced to nothing more than a bluff, work in all quarters continued. The only people who believed such an invasion was possible were the British. How else to explain the expenditure in men, money, and matériel by the Germans?

In the center of this superfluous activity was Adolf Hitler, whose eyes had already turned toward the east. Yet he continued with the charade. Hitler's July 16 directive detailed the requirements for a successful cross-Channel invasion. These included absolute mastery of the skies by the Luftwaffe. The RAF had to be reduced to a level that did not threaten an invasion fleet. The Channel crossing routes would have to be free of mines and the entrances to the Channel on both ends would have to blocked with dense mine fields to keep British warships out. Shortly before the invasion the British naval forces would have to be tied down by German naval action in the North Sea. This latter plan failed to recognize the fact that the German navy was incapable of massing a fleet of warships strong enough to fight the British Home Fleet even in a delaying action.

Little attention was paid to the preparations for the invasion by any of the principal participants. The only commander who actually responded to Hitler in a positive manner was Göring, who gave a contemptuous shrug of his shoulders, indicating that of course his air force would control the skies over Britain.

Gradually the idea of an invasion receded, and another

approach to the problem of Britain gained prominence. This called for bringing the British people to their knees by a U-boat blockade and a relentless bombing campaign. Göring, still stung by the failure of his air force at Dunkirk, sought to redeem himself by taking on the task of destroying the RAF and mastering the skies over Britain. So began the Battle of Britain.

While it is obvious to all that a delayed cross-Channel invasion of Britain was doomed to failure, even if the Germans had taken it seriously, the question must inevitably be asked: Was there a time when a German invasion of Britain could have succeeded?

In his history of the planning and preparations for Operation Sea Lion, Peter Fleming provides an excellent response.

There can be no doubt as to when a German invasion would have had the best prospects of success. Had the Germans been able to put quite a small force—say three or four divisions—across the Channel early in June (that "very dark hour," as Churchill called it two years later) they might have done the trick. The reinforcement, and indeed the maintenance, of this force would have presented serious difficulties, but some of these could have been overcome by the capture of airfields in south-east England, which in those days would not have been a hard task.[26]

Perhaps without realizing it, Fleming was endorsing General Milch's original proposal for an immediate air-launched invasion of Britain in the first week of June. Milch's first objective was the capture of airfields by paratroopers flown in on transport planes; then the troops would fan out across the southern part of the country and rush to seize London.

An attack on southern England during early June would have had a devastating effect on a nation that was virtually defenseless. But the opportunity to win such a great victory was lost because Hitler could not decide how he wanted to deal with the British. He refused to understand Churchill's clear signals that Britain would fight on against Germany even after the loss of her ally France. These were brave words from a nation that had good reason to doubt the security of the traditional protection afforded by the English Channel.

Had Hitler acted decisively after Dunkirk, and not waited to see if the British would come to terms with him, he likely would have succeeded in conquering Britain. Without the British Isles as a base of operations, U.S. troops would have had no place to train and from which to launch an invasion of the European continent. Without the British army, there would have been no one to oppose the Italians and Germans in North Africa. The United States could not have engaged in a real war against Germany without the British islands and army as allies.

4

THE VICTORY THAT ALMOST WAS

We didn't win the Battle of Britain, they lost it.
Sir Christopher Foxley Norris
RAF Air Chief Marshal

Hermann Göring was made a *Reichsmarschall*, the equivalent of a six-star general, only the second in German history. Hitler evidently decided to overlook Göring's failure to destroy the British army at Dunkirk in what the obese Nazi officer had boasted would be the Luftwaffe's "finest hour."

Again foolishly ignoring past performance for empty promise, Hitler believed Göring's pledge that his Luftwaffe would be master of the skies over Great Britain. In fact, the Battle of Britain crippled the German air force so severely that it never fully regained its earlier strength.

While Hitler nurtured the hollow hope that Britain was preparing to come to terms, the Luftwaffe conducted regular attacks against ships headed toward Britain. Indicative of the shaky condition of the RAF was that sometimes the Germans encountered stiff resistance from Spitfires and Hurricanes, and at other times their attacks on merchant shipping went uncontested.

The Battle of Britain, which was almost exclusively an air war between German and British pilots, was staged in three phases. The first phase took place primarily over the English Channel. The second phase was a challenge duel between the Luftwaffe and the RAF, intended by the Germans to be a death blow to the RAF. The third phase changed the complexion of the battle entirely as Hitler turned his air strength against British cities and civilians in retaliation for the British bombing of German cities. This shift in policy altered the outcome of the battle and ultimately robbed the Luftwaffe of its greatest victory.

July 10, 1940, is generally considered to be the beginning of the Battle of Britain. In the early morning of that rain-filled day, German bombers attacked shipping in the English Channel while their fighter escorts engaged British fighters in deadly combat. In this first phase of the Battle of Britain the Germans had two major objectives. The first was to halt the arrival in Britain of food and war matériel being shipped from abroad, especially the United States. The second was to entice the British Fighter Command to commit its limited number of fighter planes to battles over the Channel with the numerically superior German fighter units. Had the British taken the bait, it is likely that most of the planes and pilots which defended British cities later that summer would have been lost in this initial phase.

The survival of the British fighter squadrons was owed directly to the brilliance of their commander, Air Chief Marshal Sir Hugh Dowding. He was determined, at whatever risk during this critical period, to hold some of his fighters in reserve. Had he not done so, the loss of British fighter planes, and their more valuable and less readily replaced pilots, would have had a disastrous effect on the outcome of the battle.

As far as Göring was concerned, there was to be no invasion of Britain. The British would be brought to their knees by his air superiority. All he had to do was draw the British fighters out over the Channel and destroy them.

This first phase of the Battle of Britain lasted until mid-August and accomplished little for either side, except that British manufacturing facilities were steadily increasing their production of fighters while Germany's production remained static.

Less than 40,000 tons of shipping was lost to the German attacks in the Channel. The RAF, which had begun the battle with about 700 Spitfires and Hurricanes as its main instrument of defense, lost 70 fighters during this initial phase. The Luftwaffe lost 180 planes out of some 2,670 fighters and bombers.

A factor that loomed large in this and the later phases of the battle was that the majority of German pilots forced to crash-land or parachute from their planes either landed in Britain, where they were imprisoned, or drowned in the Channel. Few were able to fly their crippled planes back to the Continent. The fate of British pilots forced down was distinctly different. Since they were flying over the English countryside or close to its shores, they could easily return to their units to fly again.

Having failed to lure large numbers of British fighters out over the Channel to engage in combat, Göring decided to take the battle to the RAF directly. On August 12, 1940, the Luftwaffe launched the second phase of the Battle of Britain with a large-scale bombing attack on six British radar facilities. Radar had become important to the British defenders because it enabled them to spot incoming bombers at great distances and alert the fighter squadrons to meet them. In that first surprise raid, five radar facilities were damaged and one destroyed.

On the following two days German bombers pounded RAF airfields. Göring's aim was to destroy the British fighters—if not in combat in the air, then while they were on the ground. As part of that goal he wanted to render as many British airfields as possible unusable or inoperative. "I will smash their fighter defenses in four days," he bragged.[1]

This second phase of the Battle of Britain was different from anything the Germans had done to date. The army, the main instrument of Germany's war effort, was not involved in the battle at all. While German U-boats continued to stalk British shipping on the high seas, the focus of the battle was strictly in the air.

Also missing from this campaign was a clear military objective, other than a vague plan to wear down the RAF. Every ranking German had his personal opinion of why the battle was being waged and what would be accomplished if victory was achieved. Few, if any, believed the air war would lead to an invasion of Britain.

The Battle of Britain was unique in another respect. The British pilots, through their skill, tenacity, and courage, impressed the German pilots that they were their equals. The German flyers respected the British pilots, and the two fought what can only be described as a chivalrous battle, much like two armies of knights meeting on a grassy plain for honorable combat.

Luftwaffe General Werner Kreipe describes an incident that typifies the almost comradely attitude shared by the pilots of both nations.

[British] Squadron Leader [Douglas] Bader had lost both legs before the war, but had overcome this great handicap [through the use of artificial legs] and was now a fighter ace. He was shot down near St. Omer and his aluminum legs were smashed. That evening he was entertained in the officers' mess of Colonel Galland's wing. Squadron Leader Bader said that he wondered if there were any means whereby the spare pair he possessed in England could be sent to him. Galland got in touch with me—I was chief operations officer at Third Air Fleet at the time—and I spoke to Field Marshal Sperrle. With the Field Marshal's approval we sent a message by wireless, using the international emergency wave length, and within forty-eight hours the Squadron leader's artificial legs came floating down by parachute on to St. Omer airfield.[2]

The Battle of Britain was unique for several other reasons. Each contributed to the defeat of the Luftwaffe and each is tied inexorably to Hitler's indecisiveness concerning his policy toward Great Britain. The first was the lack of a clear objective other than destroying the RAF and hoping in some way to wear down the morale of the British people.

Hitler knew enough about the British to realize they were substantially different from the French. Britons were not going to let bombing and naval attacks wear them down, just as, later in the war, the Allies should have understood that the terror bombing of German cities would stiffen German resolve, not weaken it. In that respect Hitler's belief in the similarity of the German and British peoples was correct.

German pilots were sent each day to fight an enemy that their own commander, Göring, and his commander, Hitler, really did not want to fight. Each step Hitler took toward escalating the war with Britain, at least at this stage, was done with great reluctance.

As late as August 18, 1940, in the midst of the Battle of Britain, Hitler persisted in his reluctance. He told Vidkun Quisling, "I now find myself forced against my will to fight this war against Britain. I find myself in the same position as Martin Luther, who had just as little desire to fight Rome but was left with no alternative."[3]

Göring was also a reluctant warrior. He had never wanted war with Britain and had tried so many times to find a way to establish peace with the British that Foreign Minister Joachim von Ribbentrop complained the Luftwaffe chief was interfering in foreign affairs.

During the period of the "phony war" following the fall of Poland and before the invasion of France, Göring had maintained a clandestine communications link with British Prime

Minister Neville Chamberlain. This was an unusual, if not unheard-of, situation because both countries were officially at war with each other. Even after the Battle of Britain was lost, Göring attempted to find a means of settling things with Britain. In early June 1941 he sent word to the British that Hitler planned to invade Russia within weeks.

Thus, the two men who controlled the German air force, Hitler and Göring, were fighting a war they did not want to fight against an enemy they both sincerely wanted as an ally. As the summer of 1940 passed into autumn, Hitler pursued his reluctant war at a fearful cost of both the lives of experienced and courageous pilots and airplanes that German industry was hard put to replace. Both would be sorely missed the following year in the skies over the Soviet Union. The lives of those men were literally thrown away in a senseless campaign. Ironically, while their leaders were hesitant, the men in combat—the pilots of the German fighters and bombers—almost succeeded in winning Hitler's reluctant war.

On August 13, 1,485 German planes swept across the English Channel and attacked Britain. The following day bad weather reduced the number of attackers to 500. By the end of the third day, August 15, 190 German planes had been lost. The British lost 115 fighters in the same period.[4] While the number of German planes and pilots lost was greater, the percentages worked to Britain's disadvantage.

Even though Britain was producing more fighters than Germany, the real challenge to Britain was manning the fighter squadrons with adequately trained pilots. By August 16, Dowding's Fighter Command had already fallen below minimum acceptable strength by 209 pilots. The average life expectancy of a British fighter pilot was now less than 87 flying hours. Exhaustion took a heavy toll on the survivors; many of them routinely fell asleep as they taxied their aircraft to a stop. It was not uncommon for ground crew members to remove a sleeping pilot from his plane when he returned from combat.[5]

The overall condition of Fighter Command is described by General Sir Hastings Ismay, Churchill's chief of staff, as he recalled watching one day's air combat being plotted in Fighter Command's Operations Room: "There had been heavy fighting throughout the afternoon; and at one moment every single squadron in the group was engaged; there was nothing in reserve, and the map table showed new waves of attackers crossing the coast. I felt sick with fear."[6]

Dowding's Fighter Command finally got relief on August 17, but it was of questionable value. Men who were trained to fly the Fairey-Battle day bombers would supplement his fighter pilot force. While these replacement pilots meant more fighter planes in the skies, it also meant greater losses. These men, most of whom had never fired an aircraft's guns, received less than two weeks of training before going into combat. Their fate was black indeed, as evidenced by the example of two sergeants who reported for duty to the 111th Squadron at Croydon early one morning. Before they could unpack their luggage, they were sent up against a German attack. By 5 P.M. that evening one was dead and the other in shock at a nearby hospital, unable to recall his name. Outside the 111th's mess hall their car remained parked, still loaded with their luggage.[7]

On the same day Dowding received word of the additional pilots, a top-secret survey reported that 3,851 British pilots had been killed or reported missing since the war began. That was almost as many casualties as the army had suffered. Some 4,400 soldiers had been lost, including those who had fought across Belgium and France. It was obvious to many that Britain could not continue to sustain such losses much longer.

As Operation Sea Lion and all hope of an invasion of Britain evaporated, the air war continued. Costs mounted heavily on both sides. The lumbering German bombers were sitting ducks for the swift, maneuverable Spitfires and Hurricanes, and the German fighters were limited to an average of ten minutes of combat before they had to turn back to the Continent if they were to have any hope of landing at a friendly airfield. It was a war of attrition that exacted heavy tolls on both sides.

The beginning of what should have been the end for the RAF was on August 24. German attacks had knocked out six important communications centers and five Fighter Command airfields. In the next 14 days 460 British fighters were lost, compared with 215 German fighters and 140 German bombers. Much more devastating was the loss through death or serious injury of fully one-fourth of all RAF fighter pilots. Even the indomitable Winston Churchill felt Britain's organized air defense could survive only a few weeks more.[8]

By September 7 the RAF fighter reserve had plummeted from a high of 518 to a perilously low 292 aircraft. For the first time since the war began, Britain's aircraft industry could not keep pace with the number of fighters being lost. The average fighter squadron had only 16 of the 26 pilots it required.[9]

The second phase of the Battle of Britain was working. The Fighter Command of the RAF, while still able to fight off bomber attacks and wage relentless dogfights with German fighters, was nearing the end of its ability to control the skies over Britain. Then, Adolf Hitler again came to Britain's rescue.

As so frequently happens throughout human history, an accident changed the course of the Battle of Britain and the course of the war. Throughout this phase of the campaign, German bombers attacked military airfields, aircraft factories, and other strategic targets that provided support for Fighter Command's defense system. Strict orders from Hitler himself forbade attacking any civilian targets, especially the city of London. On the night of August 23 that prohibition was inadvertently violated.

During an unusual night bombing raid aimed at aircraft factories and fuel storage facilities near London, the navigator of the lead aircraft made an error in his calculations, causing a flight of 12 bombers to drop their bombs on London itself. Nine civilians were killed. In retaliation British bombers attacked Berlin several times during the following week.

On September 4, Hitler warned that if the British continued to bomb Berlin, he would have no choice but to level their cities. He promised a gathering of women, mostly nurses and social workers, that should Britain increase attacks on German cities, he would "raze their cities to the ground." He then raised the specter of an invasion as a veiled threat should Britain continue bombing German civilians. "The people in England are very curious, and they ask: 'Why doesn't he come?' We answer: Calm yourselves! Calm yourselves! He is coming!"[10]

The British bombers continued to attack German cities. Their raids caused negligible damage and slight loss of life, but it was loss of face that disturbed Hitler. By now he realized his boasts about invading Britain were coming to nothing. There would be no invasion, and that would be a mortal embarrassment. Added to this humiliation was the fact that British bombers seemed capable of attacking German cities almost at will. He could stand no more.

At what many believe was the very moment the RAF Fighter Command was about to collapse from exhaustion and lack of qualified pilots, Hitler ordered a change in tactics. No longer would the Luftwaffe's goal be the destruction of the fighter units; now it would be the destruction of the British cities. The English would pay for humiliating Hitler. He would break their morale by destroying their homes and businesses instead of their aircraft.

Opinion among the Luftwaffe leaders concerning the change in policy was mixed. Field Marshal Hugo Sperrle, commander of the Third Air Fleet, believed that Fighter Command was still a strong force that must be dealt with before changing tactics. Field Marshal Albert Kesselring, commander of the Second Air Fleet, thought the change would spell the end for Fighter Command. Kesselring had listened to the bragging of some of his pilots about their successful dogfights and the resultant decline in enemy fighters sent against the attackers. He expressed the opinion that Fighter Command would hold back its reserve rather than continue to fight under the existing unfavorable circumstances. The best way to destroy Fighter Command, he argued, was to attack a target so critically important that the British would be compelled to defend it with every plane they had.

Göring was unsure that the switch in strategy was advisable. While he still held out hope that peace could be made with Britain, he realized the Luftwaffe was being decimated in the air war, as was the RAF, and he sought a way out of the situation. He also knew that bombing London would end all hope of a peaceful settlement between Germany and Britain, and the goal of breaking British morale could not be accomplished by bombing their cities.

"Do you think that Germany would cave in if Berlin was wiped out?" Göring asked General Hans Jeschonnek, who supported Hitler's new bombing policy. "Of course not!" Jeschonnek snapped. Then he realized Göring had drawn him into a trap with his analogy between German and British resolve. "British morale is more brittle than our own," Jeschonnek quickly retorted.

Göring knew better. "That's where you are wrong."[11]

Hitler's decision to change the Luftwaffe's direction from the destruction of Fighter Command to the bombing of London and other cities was as ill-timed as his other major blunders. Historian Edwin Hoyt is of the opinion that the Luftwaffe was "within perhaps twenty-four hours of victory—one more immense raid on the fighter sectors might have done the job—but he had stopped; now it was impossible to regain the lost momentum."[12]

"It was a mistake. For the Luftwaffe was within sight of victory," wrote Allen Andrews in his history of the air war. He then explained why the decision to change targets was a mistake.

Between 24 August and 6 September the German Air Force had discovered the key to conquest and inflicted tremendous damage on Fighter Command through sustained attacks on its sector stations and airfields. The British defense was failing, not only through exhaustion but also through the loss of technical efficiency due to the battering of its prized system of fighter control.[13]

Fighter Command was staggering under the blows delivered by the Luftwaffe. No longer were the British fighter pilots racking up impressive victories in the skies. When the Battle of Britain began, the quick little Spitfires and Hurricanes were downing three German aircraft for each one they lost. That ratio was now reduced to one for one. With production slowed and reserves dropping rapidly, Fighter Command could not continue fighting on these terms for more than a week, perhaps two at the most.

In his account of the Battle of Britain, Winston Churchill called the decision to abandon bombing Fighter Command targets "a foolish mistake."

They were getting terribly knocked about, and their runways were ruined by craters. It was therefore with a sense of relief that Fighter Command felt the German attack turn on to London on September 7, and concluded that the enemy had changed his plan. Goering should certainly have persevered against the airfields, on whose organization and combination the whole fighting power of our air force at this moment depended.[14]

The Battle of Britain, in its new phase, continued for months. The switch in targets from airfields and aircraft factories to cities and populations spelled doom for the

Luftwaffe. Fighter Command was given a reprieve that provided the vitally needed time to rest its experienced pilots, train new pilots, and receive delivery of new planes at an ever increasing rate. By spring the German attacks on British cities had slackened to a trickle as Luftwaffe units were transferred east for the coming invasion of the Soviet Union.

5

STUMBLING TO MOSCOW

Had the cards been played differently, Hitler
might have been the Napoleon who
marched beyond Moscow.
                                                    Ronald Lewin

In the quiet predawn hours of Sunday, June 22, 1941, a train carrying grain and oil from the Soviet Union crossed into German-occupied Poland on its way to Nazi Germany. The delivery was being made in accordance with a treaty between Hitler and Stalin. A short time later, at 3:15 A.M., 6,000 German cannons opened fire on Soviet positions along an 1,800-mile front. Within an hour three German armies swept across the border and plunged headlong toward the Russian heartland.

In the first hours of the invasion of the Soviet Union, called Operation Barbarossa after the twelfth-century Holy Roman Emperor Frederick I, who was known as Redbeard or Barbarossa, 66 Soviet airfields were attacked by German bombers. By the end of the first day 1,000 Soviet aircraft were destroyed, many while still on the ground. This represented one-quarter of the entire Soviet air strength. In the next six days five Russian armies were defeated.

The invasion was conducted by three army groups, each with its own set of goals and objectives. The northern group, under Field Marshal Wilhelm von Leeb, crossed from East Prussia into Soviet-occupied Lithuania and drove toward Leningrad; the center group, under Field Marshal Fedor von Bock, swept across northern Poland and headed for Smolensk, 200 miles west of Moscow; the southern group, led by Field Marshal Gerd von Rundstedt, pushed into Galicia on its way through the Ukraine to seize Kiev.

The Soviet reaction to the invasion was almost total confusion. In spite of intelligence reports warning of an impending attack, which were supported by observation of large German troop movements to the frontier, Stalin and his military commanders appear to have been totally bewildered. When they finally did react, their response to the invasion was tentative and indecisive.

Four hours after the German attack, as Soviet field commanders desperately radioed Moscow for instructions, Marshal Georgi Zhukov relayed Stalin's directive authorizing Soviet troops to "attack the enemy and destroy him." The directive limited Soviet forces to attacking only those German units which had actually crossed the frontier. Under no circumstances were they themselves to cross the border. Soviet pilots were allowed to cross the frontier into German territory, but were limited to attacking targets less than 150 kilometers from the border. The Soviet people were not told about the invasion until Foreign Minister Vyacheslav Molotov announced it during a radio broadcast at noon.

What followed was more than four years of total war waged between two tyrants whose low regard for human life, even the lives of their countrymen, is unequaled in modern history. The tenor of the war was established on the very first day when advancing German troops under General von

Manstein found the mutilated bodies of a German patrol the Soviets had captured and executed. It was obvious from the condition of the bodies that the German soldiers had been tortured before they died. This was to be a war of unrelenting terror on both sides.

The Soviet defenders were spread in a thin line along the frontier. Actually they appeared to be more an army prepared to begin an invasion than one preparing to defend against an invasion. Although the Soviet defenses were stronger than they anticipated, Hitler's armies lunged forward at surprising speed, one victory rapidly following another.

By the end of the first day, Pruzhany and Kobryn, two important towns in the fortress area of the frontier, were in German hands. Although many Soviet units fought gallantly, they were handicapped by their lack of preparedness and the confusion that prevailed throughout the Soviet chain of command. The extent of this confusion was apparent in an absurd directive issued by Soviet General Semyon Timoshenko shortly after 9 P.M. on the first day, his third since the invasion began that morning. Timoshenko ordered Soviet frontier forces to attack across the border and secure German territory to a depth of between 50 and 75 miles. This at a time when Soviet forces were being scattered, slaughtered, and taken prisoner at a dizzying pace.

By June 26 the armored spearhead of Field Marshal von Leeb's army reached Dvinsk, 185 miles inside Soviet territory, and captured the important rail and road bridges across the Dvina River. The following day two panzer groups of Field Marshal von Bock's center army encircled 350,000 Soviet soldiers east of the city of Minsk. Almost all of those caught in the trap were killed or captured.

In a desperate move calculated to stem the German advance, Stalin issued an order establishing the "scorched earth" policy that would accompany Soviet retreats for months to come. The directive required that any Red Army

unit withdrawing from a town or city remove with it everything that could move, including rail equipment, food, and
cattle. Anything that could not be removed was to be destroyed. The Germans were not to be left a single locomotive,
not a truck, not a loaf of bread, not a liter of fuel.

Each day brought more German victories and Soviet de-
feats, except for several occasions when Red Army forces
temporarily stalled the invaders. On June 29 the Galician city
of Lvov was captured. The Soviet secret police, the NKVD,
slaughtered 3,000 Ukrainian political prisoners before withdrawing. As the Soviets fell back, Ukrainian nationalists
began a massacre of Jews, whom they accused of supporting
the communists.

On July 1 the Germans seized the Latvian city of Riga.
Later that month Smolensk fell after being surrounded by
von Bock's army. Von Rundstedt's forces entered Kiev on
September 19, and 660,000 Soviet soldiers were taken prisoner as a result of a pincer movement that trapped them
without chance of escape. The Crimea was cut off from the
rest of Russia by the capture of Perekop on September 27.

At first blush the German invasion of the Soviet Union appeared to be a stunning success, with one victory after another as Hitler's forces pushed relentlessly east. But the
invasion carried with it the seeds of its own defeat: Hitler's
personal interference in the planning and course of the campaign. By the time the Soviet invasion was launched, Hitler
had taken such complete control of the German army that
German generals mockingly joked, "You can't move the
sentry from the window to the door without Hitler's
permission."

Some of the best military minds in the West expected the
Germans to make short work of the Soviets, and for a while
they did. The chief of Britain's Imperial General Staff, General Sir John G. Dill, commented, "I suppose they [Soviet
troops] will be rounded up in hordes."[1]

While some historians look upon the invasion of the Soviet

Union as Hitler's most serious mistake, others see it differently. A prominent voice among the latter is the British military historian Ronald Lewin, who wrote that the invasion of Russia could have been "a very different proposition and though it was ruined by Hitler's own strategic decisions, the idea of Operation Barbarossa should not be too quickly or too contemptuously dismissed."[2] The war between Germany and the Soviet Union cost millions of lives. Looking back almost half a century later, it appears obvious that despite some setbacks, the German army would most likely have carried the campaign if not for the meddling of Adolf Hitler.

Hitler committed two of his costliest blunders before the invasion ever started. The first was launching a military operation of massive proportions while the German army was insufficiently prepared for such an ambitious undertaking, and then compounding the error by failing to understand the importance of Moscow as a primary target for the invasion forces.

From the very beginning of his military ventures, Hitler never provided his army enough time or money to prepare fully for the campaigns he sent them to fight. Each time he issued the orders to march, his generals were almost unanimous in their warnings that the troops were unprepared to fight. They always needed more men, more money, and more training. Hitler's confidence in himself as a bold military leader was created at the expense of his confidence in the generals, who always seemed to counsel caution.

The generals preached caution when he marched into the Rhineland, and the Allies did nothing. They urged caution when he took Czechoslovakia, and the Allies did nothing. They urged caution when he attacked Poland, and he conquered that country with relative ease and speed. Once again they urged caution when he attacked the countries of western Europe, including France, and his armies swept through to the Atlantic in incredible time. With that kind of track record it is easy to understand why Hitler saw himself as a better military leader than his generals. The one thing he overlooked was that much of his success was a direct result of the inactions or errors of his opponents rather than his ability as a master strategist or tactician.

The invasion of the Soviet Union paralleled Hitler's earlier invasions with regard to the lack of overall preparedness. But this failing would have a dramatically different effect on both the war against the Soviet Union and the survival of the Third Reich.

In 1941 the German army contained 21 panzer divisions, which on the surface amounted to a doubling of the number of panzer divisions over the previous year. That numerical increase was actually achieved through the dilution of the existing units. For example, during the earlier campaign in the West, a panzer division was composed of a core of a tank brigade made up of two regiments with a total of slightly over 300 operational tanks. Before the Soviet invasion each division lost one regiment, about 150 tanks. This resulted in more divisions, but fewer tanks and a greatly reduced fighting strength for each division. Each division now contained fewer than 2,600 tank personnel of its contingent of 17,000 soldiers. The rest were unarmored auxiliary troops and larger regimental staffs.

As far as Hitler was concerned, the little tank symbols on his situation maps represented panzer divisions. He didn't care that they were now half the strength they once were; he expected the same accomplishments as if they were at full strength. One of his greatest weaknesses as a military leader was his obsession with numbers of fighting units. If his high command flunkies could find a way to put more little tank symbols on his maps, then he could use the power of his will to force a division fighting at half strength to accomplish what it could have done at full strength.

On the day of the invasion, when the armored divisions were to play as important a part as they had the year before in France and the Low Countries, Germany had fewer than

4,000 tanks in operation. Most of these were older models slated for replacement. Almost 20 percent of them had been taken from the defeated Czech army. Only 1,400 of the German tanks were the newer Mark III and Mark IV models.

Despite the pleas of the experienced tank commander, General Heinz Guderian, to provide the invasion forces with tracked vehicles for the transportation of men and supplies inside the Soviet Union, where paved roads were practically nonexistent, the invading army depended on standard trucks and horse-drawn wagons and carts for its supplies. Some 650,000 horses were used for transport by this army that made such effective use of tanks. Just as they had in the time of Napoleon's invasion, the horses died by the thousands when the frozen snow covered the ground and they could not break through in search of forage.

As a result of the dilution of its tank strength, the average German panzer division was comprised of nearly ten times as many wheeled vehicles as tracked vehicles. This heavy reliance on wheeled vehicles was of less importance in the western campaign, where enemy forces collapsed under the surprise attack and there was an abundance of paved roads for the attacking forces to use. Conditions were not the same in the Soviet Union, as British military historian B. H. Liddell Hart pointed out.

But in the East, where proper roads were scarce, it proved a decisive brake in the long run. The Germans here paid the penalty for being, in practice, twenty years behind the theory which they had adopted as their key to success.[3]

Part of Germany's unpreparedness for the requirements of a war in the Soviet Union resulted from the lack of reliable intelligence about the enemy. It is difficult to find a similar circumstance where such a grand military enterprise was undertaken with so little knowledge of the enemy's military strength and resolve. Hitler deluded himself into believing the Soviet Union would simply collapse under the weight of a blitzkrieg. This attitude was summed up in one sentence that Hitler used repeatedly before the invasion of the Soviet Union began: "We have only to kick in the door and the whole rotten structure will come crashing down."[4]

Ironically, there was a kernel of truth in Hitler's assessment of Soviet resolve, but the Nazi conviction that the peoples of eastern Europe were inferiors who could easily be enslaved or slaughtered, played an important role in keeping the structure from crashing down.

Another result of Hitler's lack of reliance on intelligence reports concerning the enemy worked against the Soviet invasion: an almost total ignorance of the terrain over which his army would advance. The army was able to overcome this shortcoming in the invasion of France and the Low Countries by sending agents disguised as tourists into the target countries to purchase the famous Michelin maps. It was not uncommon in the spring of 1940 to find a panzer commander stopped along a French road, checking his Michelin map for directions. There were no equivalent maps for Russia. The result was that German units often would lose their way, especially during the early phases of the invasion, when the army moved forward so rapidly.

As the time for the invasion approached, Hitler ignored warnings that the Soviet army was larger and better equipped than he thought. These warnings came from several well-informed and highly reliable sources, including the Abwer, the foreign counterintelligence department of the high command, and his own representative in Moscow, Count Friedrich Werner von Schulenberg. Von Schulenberg even traveled to Berlin to put his case to Hitler directly. After giving Hitler a full report on the strength of the Soviet forces, von Schulenberg was brushed off with the comment "Thank you, this was extremely interesting." It was obvious that Hitler was unwilling to believe the Soviet Union was going to do anything other than "come crashing down."[5]

Hitler's plans for the invasion overlooked or ignored three important facts about the Soviet Union that good intelligence could forecast. First was the speed with which Stalin could mobilize the population and the size of such a mobilization. The second was Stalin's ability to transfer troops from Siberia, where they were awaiting a Japanese attack, to replace those killed or captured by the Germans. Hitler acted as if the Soviets did not have large, well-trained armies stationed throughout Asiatic Russia. These troops were used with devastating effect against the German armies bogged down, in summer uniforms, by the worst winter in half a century.

The third, and perhaps most important, was the early development of new Soviet tanks, notably the T-34, that were superior to anything in the German arsenal. Hitler planned a tank war against an army about whose tank strength he had little or no knowledge. In a dispatch to President Franklin Roosevelt in July 1941, Stalin boasted that the Soviet Union had 24,000 tanks, of which 12,000 were in European Russia. It was against this unknown might that Hitler threw his army of less than 4,000 tanks. In addition to overwhelming numerical superiority, the Soviet T-34s, in production since 1939, were judged by many armor experts to be the best in the war. By the beginning of 1942 the T-34 dominated the battlefield, outgunning and outmaneuvering the German tanks.

When German infantrymen first confronted the T-34, they were astounded that shells from their 37-mm and 50-mm antitank guns simply bounced off the Soviet armor. The effect was devastating, as General Gunther Blumentritt describes:

At Vereya the Russian tanks simply drove straight through the 7th Infantry Division to the artillery positions and literally ran over the guns. The effect on the infantryman's morale was comprehensible. This marked the beginning of what came to be called the "tank terror."[6]

Besides being ill-prepared, Hitler's entire plan for the invasion and his goals were deficient. In the words of British historian Ronald Lewin, failure of the Russian campaign was preordained by Hitler's "decisions taken even before the campaign was launched."[7]

One of the first indications that Hitler was seriously contemplating an attack on the Soviet Union is recorded in Army Chief of Staff General Franz Halder's diary on July 22, 1940. The entry reveals the vagueness of Hitler's goals from the earliest discussions of the Soviet campaign: "To defeat the Russian army, or at least to occupy as much Russian soil as is necessary to protect Berlin from air attack, it is desired to establish our own positions so far to the east that our own air force can destroy the most important areas of Russia."[8]

In a characteristically deceitful move Hitler pitted the army general staff against the high command of the armed forces (OKW), over which he maintained total control through his flunkies General Wilhelm Keitel and General Alfred Jodl. Hitler instructed both Jodl and General Franz Halder, chief of the general staff, to prepare preliminary plans for a Soviet invasion. Halder was unaware the high command was duplicating his efforts.

Halder chose the chief of staff of the 18th Army, General Erich Marcks, to oversee the invasion planning. Jodl, operating independently of the army and in secret, ordered Baron von Lossberg to prepare his own invasion plan.

The Marcks Plan, as it became known, was accepted by the general staff and tested in a series of war games conducted between November 28 and December 3, 1940. It established three main objectives for the invasion: the area around Moscow, the region around Leningrad, and the cities of the Ukraine, the former breadbasket of Europe. The von Lossberg Plan ignored Moscow as a primary target, replacing it with Smolensk, 200 miles to the west.

On December 5 Halder presented Hitler with the Marcks Plan, fully expecting that the plan recommended by the general staff would be adopted. One can only guess at the shock and dismay Halder felt when Hitler told him, "Moscow is of no great importance." The von Lossberg Plan became the blueprint for the invasion of the Soviet Union.

The failure to recognize the importance of Moscow, not only at the beginning of the planning stage for the campaign but also later on, as the actual fighting progressed, remains one of Hitler's most glaring and far-reaching blunders of the entire war.

Completely disregarded by Hitler was the simple truth that lay behind General Marcks's statement in the conclusion of the report he prepared as part of his plan. Of the three areas he identified as important, Moscow was foremost: "Moscow contains the economic, political and spiritual center of the U.S.S.R. Its capture would destroy the coordination of the Russian State."[9]

The importance of Moscow as the heart and brain of the vast Soviet empire is magnified a hundredfold when one considers that by European standards Russia was a primitive country. This was especially true concerning communications and transportation. The Soviet Union was a totalitarian state governed by a system that depended on central control of the country, the armed forces, and the general population. The seat of the central control was Moscow. The capital was clearly the definitive primary target of the campaign. One of the greatest conflicts of opinion between Hitler and the army commanders hinged on this point. Hitler perceived the Ukraine as the most important target; the military recognized Moscow as the most critical objective. Moscow was like the hub of a great communications wheel, with its spokes going in all directions. All communications had to go through Moscow before reaching their destinations. The capture of Moscow meant the capture of the center of all civilian and military communications in the country west of the Urals.

Hitler's blunder in failing to identify Moscow as the primary military objective of the invasion was described by historian Dr. Earl F. Ziemke. "Hitler," he said, "was so intent on getting the territory that he refused to recognize that the object of war is not to take territory but to defeat the other fellow's military forces."[10]

In fairness to Hitler it must be pointed out that economic conditions as well as military strategy influenced his decisions. Germany was dependent on imports for the raw materials needed to conduct war. Everything from iron ore to tungsten and manganese had to be imported. In addition, Germany's reserves of tin and copper had been exhausted the previous year. The only vital resource Germany had in abundance was coal. The natural resources of the Caucasus and the Ukraine made them high-priority targets for Hitler.[11]

The battle plan approved by Hitler called for three army groups. The northern group was to seize Leningrad with the help of the Finnish army. The center group was provided the most armor and assigned to take Smolensk. The southern group would advance through the Ukraine and the Crimea. Its largest target was Kiev, capital of the Ukraine.

The "final objective," as Hitler planned the war, was to "erect a barrier against Asiatic Russia" along a line connecting Archangel on the White Sea to the Volga River east of Moscow, then following the river south to Astrakhan on the Caspian Sea.

Years later General Walter Warlimont, writing his memoirs, expressed the view held by most members of the general staff: "So, with a stroke of the pen, a new concept of main lines of the campaign against Russia was substituted for that which the OKH [German general staff] had worked out as a result of months of painstaking examination and crosschecking from all angles by the best military minds available."[12]

Whatever their personal feelings, the German generals did what they always did when faced by the will of Adolf Hitler: They bowed to his wishes. The planning for the invasion proceeded as directed, based on the von Lossberg Plan.

Confident that the "inferiority" of the Soviet people assured a German victory, Hitler continued to disregard warnings of any kind. They included General Halder's legitimate concern about the huge manpower reserves the Soviets could tap, and the numerical superiority of Soviet tanks.

Hitler ordered his generals to complete preparations for the invasion by May 15. Had he met this original date on schedule, it is likely that the German army's greatest enemy, the subzero weather, would not have been a factor preventing it from reaching and capturing Moscow. There are only a few months in which an invading army could operate freely on the Russian roads. This period begins when the mud from the spring thaws dries, and ends in the late fall with the onset of freezing rains.

Three main reasons are given for postponing the invasion. While there remains some doubt over their relative importance, it is clear that each contributed to the rescheduling of the attack to mid June, and finally to June 22. The first was Hitler's decision to come to the aid of the Italian dictator, Benito Mussolini.

On October 28, 1940, the Italians invaded Greece. The Greeks proved to be too tough for Mussolini's troops; the Italians not only were driven out of Greece but also were pushed far beyond the point in Albania from which they had launched their invasion. German troops would have to be sent to rescue the Italian army.

The disappointing news of Italy's defeat by the Greeks was compounded on March 27, 1941, by an unexpected complication. Two days earlier the Yugoslav Prime Minister, Dragisha Cvetkovich, signed Yugoslavia's agreement to the Tripartite Pact, linking that nation to the Axis. The Yugoslavs agreed to permit free passage through their country of German troops heading for Greece. Although Yugoslavia joined the Axis at the urging of the prince regent, Prince Paul, the general population was opposed to the move. On the morning of March 27 Cvetkovich's government was overthrown

by elements of the Yugoslav military. Prince Paul was replaced by the heir to the throne, 17-year-old King Peter. The
new head of the government was Air Force General Dushan
Simovich, who immediately renounced the Tripartite Pact.
Yugoslavia had been a German ally for less than two days.

Hitler was furious at what he considered a stab in the back
from Yugoslavia. In his fury he determined to "smash Yugoslavia militarily and as a State." He called in the ambassadors
from Bulgaria and Hungary and promised them a portion of
the spoils if their countries joined in the destruction of Yugoslavia. Hungary was promised the Yugoslav province of
Banat, and Bulgaria the province of Macedonia. The Soviet
invasion, so important to Hitler's future plans for the Reich,
would have to wait while Hitler settled scores with the Yugoslavs and rescued Italy from an embarrassing defeat at the
hands of the Greeks.

The new date for Operation Barbarossa was pushed back
to mid June. An entire month would be lost in getting
started—a month that would prove fatally costly when winter set in on the German troops trying to reach Moscow.

While some historians doubt whether the diversion of
German troops to conquer Yugoslavia and Greece, a task
they accomplished in three weeks, had an impact on the invasion of the Soviet Union, the commanders in the field disagree. Field Marshal von Kleist, who commanded the panzer
forces in the southern army group during the invasion, said
on this subject:

It is true that the forces employed in the Balkans were not large
compared with our total strength, but the proportion of tanks employed there was high. The bulk of the tanks that came under me
for the offensive against the Russian front in southern Poland had
taken part in the Balkan offensive, and needed overhaul, while
their crews needed a rest. A large number of them had driven as far
south as the Peloponnese, and had to be brought back all the way.[13]

According to B. H. Liddell Hart, Field Marshal von Rundstedt agreed that the delayed arrival of the tanks used in the Balkans hampered the preparations of the southern army group he commanded in the Soviet invasion.[14]

The weather may have played a role in delaying the invasion. Spring was late in 1941, and the swollen rivers on the Soviet side of the frontier flooded the countryside for miles around. Whether Hitler actually considered this when he rescheduled the invasion is not known. The Balkan campaign, especially Hitler's decision to occupy all of Greece, was the factor that weighed most heavily on the delay.

Of course, had Hitler not been so blindly overconfident of his ability to smash the Red Army so quickly, he might have reconsidered the postponement. It is possible that the invasion could have begun even though von Rundstedt's army had contributed so much of its armored forces to the Balkans offensive. In his history of the war Liddell Hart goes so far as to suggest that had the southern group been fighting with a reduced capacity, Hitler might have been less inclined to make one of his two biggest tactical blunders of the Russo-German war, the transfer of troops from the center group to the south.

By the middle of July the German army had made incredible advances across western Russia. On July 16 German forces began encircling the city of Smolensk and Soviet troops were retreating along the entire front. Hitler, concerned that the escaping Soviet armies could eventually regroup and counterattack, wrote on July 19 that the aim of the next operations must be "to prevent any escape of large enemy forces into the depths of the Russian territory and annihilating them."[15]

To pursue this task Hitler once again turned his objective away from capturing Moscow. He ordered the panzer units fighting with the central army group, on the road to Moscow, to be withdrawn. The panzer units under General Guderian were ordered to turn south to help the southern army encircle and trap a large Soviet force on the outskirts of Kiev. The panzers of General Hermann Hoth were sent north to aid in the attack on Leningrad.

Here the generals lost an opportunity to stand against Hitler's flawed military planning. Almost to a man the members of the general staff and the field commanders wanted to take Moscow. Guderian was convinced he could reach Moscow rapidly if no time was lost, and thus could cripple the brain of the Soviet resistance. Both General Hoth and Field Marshal von Bock, commander of the center group, agreed with him.

On August 4, 1941, Hitler visited the headquarters of von Bock's Army Group Center to assess the situation personally. Von Bock was prepared to convince Hitler of the importance of continuing on to capture Moscow by having his panzer commanders, Guderian and Hoth, present for a conference with the Führer.

In a typical display of Hitler's distrust of his military commanders, he met with each of the three men separately, so they could not gang up on him. Von Bock was first. The commander of Army Group Center tried to impress on Hitler the urgent need to maintain continued pressure on the retreating Red Army. He also urged a direct attack on Moscow. When Hitler asked von Bock when he expected his forces to enter Moscow, the field marshal quickly replied, "By the end of August."[16]

Hitler's conversations with Hoth and Guderian produced the same result. Having failed to gain backing for his plan to deplete the Army Group Center of panzers to strengthen the group fighting in the Ukraine, Hitler assembled all three and lectured them on what he saw as the strategic importance of capturing the Ukraine and the Crimea. He made no mention of his plan to transfer the panzer units. The Führer then hastily departed, leaving von Bock with no clear indication of what Hitler wanted him to do next.

Von Bock expected full support for his thrust forward, so he continued. His advance troops actually came within 160 miles of Moscow during the next weeks. Then disaster befell him. Almost daily, orders arrived transferring unit after unit south for the great drive against Kiev. Hitler not only depleted von Bock's forces, he ordered the commander to assume a defensive holding position while the war in the south was prosecuted vigorously.

Unable to accept the reasoning behind the crippling of his forces, von Bock wavered between depression and rage. Finally, in a desperate effort to halt the insanity of the transfers, he placed a telephone call to the commander in chief of the army, Field Marshal von Brauchitsch. Von Bock was unaware that von Brauchitsch had himself been arguing with Hitler over the transfers. Opposing Hitler on this question would cost von Brauchitsch his post by the end of the year.

According to the historian Alfred W. Turney, the conversation began as follows:

Von Bock: I am releasing the organizations in my command according to your instructions. I hope this will prove to be satisfactory. But I will tell you that all of this is, in my professional opinion, quite asinine. It has come to my attention that your headquarters believes that my objective is the capture of Moscow. This is untrue! My first objective is, and has been, to destroy the enemy forces, after which Moscow will fall into our hands like a ripe cherry! There is, then, only one solution on my front. Attack the enemy! Defense is absolutely out of the question! How can you expect me to repel the enemy with weakened forces? And, by the way, how long will this transfer of forces from my army group be effective? Every hour that we lose is irretrievable. We are permitting the enemy the time he needs to recover, to slip from the noose we have placed upon him. There is no doubt that the enemy will now strengthen his resistance and reorganize his defense, as he has been trying to do since the campaign began!

Von Brauchitsch: I understand all that. Your remarks are quite clear. You will understand, however, that I did not make the decision.[17]

Von Bock failed to understand that the army high command was no longer in charge of the campaign; Hitler was now directing the entire operation. On December 19, von Brauchitsch was forced to retire and Hitler assumed the post of commander in chief. Von Brauchitsch became the scapegoat for the failure to achieve victory in the first year of the Russian campaign. Hitler's willingness to shift the blame for his own failures to a competent general officer is seen in a diary entry made by Joseph Goebbels:

The Fuehrer spoke of him [von Brauchitsch] only in terms of contempt. A vain cowardly wretch who could not even appraise the situation, much less master it. By his constant interference and consistent disobedience he completely spoiled the entire plan for the eastern campaign as it was designed with crystal clarity by the Fuehrer. The Fuehrer had a plan that was bound to lead to victory.[18]

Hitler prevailed. Along with other portions of von Bock's army, Guderian's panzers headed south, where they joined von Kleist's armored units to trap over 600,000 Soviet soldiers. The battle around Kiev ended in late September and finished forever the German opportunity to capture Moscow before the onslaught of winter. The two vital months lost in the fighting around Kiev meant a two-month delay before von Bock's army could reach the capital.

Guderian's and Hoth's panzers rejoined Army Group Center, and the advance on Moscow was resumed on September 30, 1941. The only major city between Smolensk and Moscow was Vyazma. When the city fell to the advancing Germans, another 650,000 Soviet prisoners were taken. But the weather was already turning bad. Driving rain turned the dirt roads into mud so deep that even the tanks were bogged down. Then came subzero temperatures followed by snow. While the frozen mud made it easier for the tracked vehicles to move, every other form of transportation became frozen in the rutted roads.

The war in Russia dragged on. Of the two cities Hitler had identified as the soul of Soviet communism, Leningrad was surrounded but never taken, and Stalingrad was entered and bitterly contested in a terrible campaign, but never capitulated to the Germans.

When von Bock's newly reformed Army Group Center launched its attack toward Moscow, it faced a rejuvenated enemy that had profited from the respite Hitler had given them to construct strong defenses and move large numbers of troops to defend the capital. Although some German units advanced to within sight of the spires of the Kremlin, they never entered the city.

The seasonal turn in the weather signaled the beginning of the end. Hitler, having convinced himself of victory before the Russian winter began, had refused to permit preparations for shipping either winter clothing for the troops or antifreeze for the vehicles. The facts of the winter campaign have been recorded so often and in such depth as to preclude the need to repeat them here. It was a time of devastating loss for the Germans, who could not maintain active operations, beyond seeking ways and means to survive, until the following spring.

In August 1941 the German Reich reached its greatest size when German troops reached the Volga River at a point several miles north of Stalingrad. In northern Russia, Leningrad remained under siege and Moscow remained in Soviet hands. It was at this point that Hitler committed what Robert Payne called "his most fatal blunder."[19]

Now in complete control of his army, Hitler stretched it beyond its limits in order to attack Stalingrad. Flanks were either left undefended or were entrusted to unreliable troops supplied by Italy, Romania, and Hungary. Other than the armament factories located there, Stalingrad had no strategic value. The factories could have been easy targets of intensive bombing, making it unnecessary to send troops to take the city.

The struggle for Stalingrad was ultimately reduced to German and Soviet troops fighting a bitter hand-to-hand battle, street by street and building by building. Combat was so close that in many instances German soldiers occupied one floor of a building while Soviet soldiers occupied another. Thousands on both sides died in struggles to gain control of single rooms in buildings already destroyed by shelling.

The battle for Stalingrad cost 250,000 German lives, largely because of Hitler's insistence that there be no retreat from territory taken by German forces. This policy, based on his belief that the mystical power of his will could be transferred to the troops fighting a losing battle against a numerically superior and determined foe, was hardly a substitute for desperately needed supplies, reinforcements, and a realistic strategy.

In the predawn hours of November 19, 1942, Hitler argued with Army Chief of Staff General Kurt Zeitzler, who had replaced Halder because the latter had disagreed with Hitler once too often. Now Zeitzler was echoing his predecessor, telling Hitler he was wrong. Zeitzler wanted Hitler to allow the Sixth Army, under General Friedrich von Paulus, to withdraw from Stalingrad because it was in danger of being completely surrounded by superior Soviet forces that had begun counterattacking the day before. He mapped out for Hitler a withdrawal plan whereby von Paulus could pull out of the city and subsequently strike the Soviet forces from the rear, crippling their offensive. Hitler raged against Zeitzler and refused his request.

Each day the encircled German and Romanian troops were drawn into an increasingly tighter net. What everyone referred to as the Stalingrad pocket, Hitler called his "Fortress Stalingrad." Throughout the following weeks Hitler remained blind and indifferent to the fate of the men in Stalingrad. Even appeals from von Paulus that he be permitted to fight his way out of the trap were denied. The reality of the situation at Stalingrad was so far removed from Hitler's own reality that on January 30, 1943, the day before von Paulus surrendered his remaining 94,000 troops, Hitler promoted him to field marshal. Only a small number of the Germans and Romanians survived Soviet imprisonment.

Hitler's refusal to sanction the German withdrawal from Stalingrad handed the Soviets a major military and psychological victory. Stalin's generals quickly seized the initiative with determined offensives on all fronts. Until Stalingrad the German army had suffered no major defeat other than its inability to take Moscow. It had presented an invincible image to the world, but now the world knew better. Following the defeat at Stalingrad there would be no more blitzkriegs. There would be no more advances, only a steady retreat across eastern Europe until the German army was forced back to where it began in 1939: Germany itself.

At a meeting with Field Marshal von Manstein, Hitler blurted out an admission of his guilt: "I alone bear the responsibility for Stalingrad."[20]

6

FROM HEROES TO VILLAINS

The war would have been won by the
Germans and their White Russian allies,
if he had the imagination to do that.
                    Colonel Trevor N. DuPuy

One of the great ironies of World War II is that the populations of much of the territory comprising the Soviet Union
initially welcomed the German soldiers as saviors. One of
Hitler's greatest blunders is that his policies alienated those
populations and influenced people who were opposed to the
communist government in Moscow to defend it as partisans
and as regular soldiers.

Beginning with the day Hitler's legions crossed into Soviet
territory, opportunities to convert local populations into allies against the Red Army abounded. Ukrainians, White Russians, Lithuanians, Latvians, and Estonians welcomed the
German invasion with open arms. As the German army advanced through the Soviet Union, its soldiers were pleas-
antly surprised by the reception they received from large

segments of the population. Even in Russia itself German soldiers were greeted with flowers and refreshments by people who saw them as heroes who came to liberate them from their communist oppressors.

Two significant factors accounted for the warm welcome the Germans received. First is the fact that the Soviet Union, which we in the West incorrectly think of as "Russia," is a federation of 15 republics in which more than 170 different ethnic groups live. Many of these groups live in segregated areas of the country and aspire to be free from Moscow. This has been true since the early rulers of Moscovy extended their rule to neighboring states, and it continues today. The populations of the Baltic states, White Russia, and the Ukraine resented their subjugation by the Russians. Nationalist and anti-Russian feelings were, and remain, extremely strong among these peoples.

The second factor that influenced the Soviet population's attitude toward the Germans was the brutality of the communist system. Thus, even within Great Russia itself German troops found a welcome.

Still fresh in the minds of these peasant populations was the famine forced on them by Stalin in order to bring them and their aspirations under tighter control. Conservative estimates place the number of peasants who died under Stalin's starvation policy, especially among the Ukrainians and the Cossacks, at 14.5 million from 1930 through 1937.[1]

In his memoirs Boris Pasternak, best known for his novel *Doctor Zhivago*, wrote of his visit to a peasant region in the early 1930s:

What I saw could not be expressed in words. There was such inhuman, unimaginable misery, such a terrible disaster, that it began to seem almost abstract, it would not fit within the bounds of consciousness. I fell ill. For an entire year I could not write.[2]

Keeping in mind that the disaster and death inflicted on

these people was a direct, calculated result of official government policy, it is small wonder they viewed Germans as saviors when they drove out the communist forces.

One young German officer described the reception he and his men received from a local population as "astonishingly cordial." He went on to relate an incident that was repeated many thousands of times throughout the first year of the German invasion of the Soviet Union:

Entering the villages we were greeted as liberators. Except for officials of the Communist Party, practically nobody fled. The Soviet government's efforts to evacuate the population from the areas under the German threat were widely obstructed and generally a failure. The only areas in which the Soviet government succeeded in evacuating the machinery and personnel of industrial plants were all at a considerable distance from the front lines. The local population showed genuine kindness towards the German troops and pinned great hopes on our arrival. Everywhere we went we were greeted with bread and salt, the traditional Slav symbols of hospitality.[3]

Anti-Semitism was another factor that played a role, albeit a less significant one, in the friendship shown the invading Germans. In addition to the historical anti-Semitism prevalent throughout the territories of the Soviet Union, many people, especially the peasants who suffered such great losses during the enforced famine, identified the Jews as part of the communist apparatus. While the deportation and murder of Jews disgusted some people in the territory occupied by Germany, large segments of the population cheered the SS and the Gestapo, even joining in as volunteer executioners and concentration camp guards.

Although anti-Semitism was widespread among the Soviet populations, not everyone agreed with the Nazi policy of extermination. Many dissidents paid with their lives, as did a group of White Russians on July 18, 1941. After being forced

to dig a large pit that would become their mass grave, a group
of 45 Jews were tied together and thrown in by their SS tor-
mentors. The Germans ordered a group of 30 White Russians
to shovel earth over the Jews. When they refused, the SS
men executed the White Russians as well. All 75 people were
left dead in the pit.[4]

The horrors visited on the populations inside the Soviet
Union for so many years blinded them to the atrocities the
Nazis would visit on them. Historian Robert Leckie reports
that the reception given the German troops was "moving":

In every village they had been showered with bouquets of flowers
even more beautiful than those they had received in Vienna. Many
villages had flower decorated triumphal arches, bearing the in-
scription in Russian and German: "The Ukranian peoples thank
their liberators, the brave German Army. Heil Adolf Hitler."[5]

Ukrainians and White Russians were not the only Soviet
peoples to welcome the German army. The Cossacks did so,
too. Not only did they welcome them, many joined the German army in its fight against the Red Army. Typical of the
Cossack reaction to the German invasion was that of Major
Ivan Nikitich Kononov, commander of the 436th Regiment.
On August 22, 1941, Kononov and his entire regiment defected to the German side after having launched a successful
counterattack against them. Kononov's was the first of many
Cossack units to change sides in the war. By the fall of 1942
more than 200 Cossack battalions and regiments fought
alongside the German army.[6]

The welcome mat was out all along the front in the western provinces of the Soviet Union. Poles and Balts from Esto-
nia, Latvia, and Lithuania hailed the Germans. Historian
Roland Gaucher describes scenes that were typical along the
entire German advance:

In the cities and villages of the Ukraine the local authorities proffered bread and salt to the conquerors. In Volhynia Bishop Polycarp Sikorsky of Vladimir issued statements favorable to the Third Reich. In all the Baltic states a vast surge of hope sent everyone into the streets to greet the German soldiers with flowers— everyone who had not been carried off by the Russians in their retreat. The bishops of Mittau, Narva, and Kaunas and the Metropolitan of Lithuania sent Hitler a telegram expressing their joy at being "liberated" from the Soviet yoke. Everywhere volunteers tried to enlist in the German army.[7]

Here was a virtually unprecedented opportunity. An invading army was welcomed by the population, and tens of thousands of young men were eager to join the invaders to fight against their own central government. Some Germans, especially field commanders, realized the awesome potential of permitting these Soviet citizens to join them. Many allowed them to take noncombatant roles despite orders to the contrary from Berlin.

The most significant defection from the Red Army during the war was that of General Andrey Andreyevich Vlasov, one of Stalin's favorite generals. He had earned the dictator's trust enough to have been assigned responsibility for the defense of the Moscow central front against von Bock's Army Group Center. As a reward for his successful defense of Moscow, Vlasov was awarded the Order of the Red Banner and promoted.

At the time of his capture, July 12, 1942, Vlasov was acting commander of the northwest front and commander of the Second Shock Army. He had had misgivings about Stalin and his dictatorship for some time. This eventually led him, after his capture, to work among the Russian POWs to raise an army to fight alongside the Germans. It was named the Russian Army of Liberation. Vlasov's unit was formed in spite of Hitler's opposition, and its activities were constantly hampered by Hitler and other high-ranking Nazis who clung to the master race philosophy.

When the war in the Soviet Union turned against Hitler, he called on Italy, Hungary, Romania, Finland, and Croatia to send more troops to the front. As usual, he was impressed by numbers. These additional units convinced him victory could be snatched from defeat. He refused to acknowledge that these units were composed of men who fought only halfheartedly. Most German field commanders found these allies unreliable and, as often as not, liable to flee when the fighting was most heavy. On the other hand, many of the units composed of Cossacks, Ukrainians, and other peoples of the Soviet Union proved to be more reliable. There could have been millions more of these men available to the German army except for the racial policies of the Nazi Party.

Mostly buried in the millions of pages written about World War II is the fact that Hitler threw away a real opportunity to defeat Stalin by his insistence that the "eastern peoples" were subhumans who could not be allowed to fight by the side of the German soldiers.

Field Marshal von Manstein, who played a crucial role in the Soviet campaign, explained the important opportunity the Germans missed in retaining the goodwill of the Soviet population:

[Hitler] based everything on the assumption that the Soviet Union could be overthrown by military means in one campaign. Had this even been possible, it could have been achieved only by bringing about the Soviet Union's simultaneous collapse from within. Yet the policies which Hitler—in complete negation of the efforts of the military authorities—pursued through his Reich Commissioners and Security Service (SD) in the occupied territories of the east were bound to achieve the very opposite effect. In other words, while his strategic policy was to demolish the Soviet system with the utmost dispatch, his political actions were diametrically opposed to this. The result was that his political measures in the east ran entirely counter to the requirements of his strategy, depriving it of whatever chance it may have had of a speedy victory.[8]

The "political measures" to which von Manstein refers were persecution, forced labor, and even extermination of the peoples of the Soviet Union. Had the Soviet population been treated more mercifully by the invader, the German forces fighting the Red Army would have been swollen many times over with Soviet deserters.

Precise figures concerning the number of Russian and other Soviet citizens who actually took up arms or found other ways to support the German army are not readily available. However, some idea of the strength of these forces is gained from the following report by historian Mark R. Elliott:

By the end of 1942 the Wehrmacht employed about 500,000 ex–Red Army men in its antiguerrilla operations, most of them apparently Russian. They varied enormously in education, in political persuasion, and in temperament; but they detested the Soviet regime and had resigned themselves to their dangerous profession only with the realization that the war's cruel circumstances offered few choices.[9]

Ironically, the man who is credited with creating the philosophical myth of the master race often supported the Soviet populations that sought to establish independent states. Alfred Rosenberg was appointed minister for occupied territories by Hitler. For years Rosenberg had preached the need for an independent Ukraine, as well as independence for other Soviet republics. Unfortunately, Rosenberg never gained Hitler's ear or his respect, so his positions were ignored.

Rosenberg's authority was so severely limited that he could not even name the commissioner who would rule each occupied territory; Hitler retained that right for himself. The Führer made his attitude concerning an independent Ukraine abundantly clear when he selected a brutal railroad worker named Erich Koch as *Reichkomissar* for the Ukraine.

Koch believed "Ukrainians are nothing but primitive Slavs. They will be ruled by the knout and vodka."[10]

The events in the Ukraine are typical of what happened as Soviet territory fell to the Germans. Behind the German army came the SS death squads. First they set about murdering Jews and communists. Any others who violated even the smallest German rule faced the same fate.

Next grain was confiscated and shipped to Germany in such quantities that nothing remained for the peasants, who were left to starve. In many areas the inefficient farm collectives were left in place because the Nazis thought the Soviet system allowed them greater control. In desperation many peasants became partisans who attacked German patrols and harassed German supply lines. Some experts believe the mistreatment and starvation of the peoples of the occupied territories caused Hitler to lose the war.

The brutality of Erich Koch and the other commissioners of the occupied territories was legend. Under their rule millions of Soviet people were killed or shipped as slave laborers to work in German industry. The net result of Nazi rule in the occupied territories of the Soviet Union was that one brutal, murderous regime was replaced by another. Hitler missed the opportunity to enlist these people in his war against Stalin. Had he done so, the result would have been different.

Many casual observers in the West have a romantic picture of the Red Army soldier fighting bravely to defend the Soviet Union against the German invaders. The image is not entirely accurate. Red Army soldiers were on average probably as courageous as soldiers from any other nation, but they, too, had suffered at the hands of Stalin and his murderers. Predictably, tens of thousands of them defected to the German side, anticipating a Nazi victory that would free them from the communist yoke.

General Wladyslaw Anders, commander of the Free Polish Army of the London-based Polish government-in-exile, described what he called the widespread disinclination of the Soviet soldier to fight in defense of the "fatherland of the proletariat", and his hatred of the regime. Many soldiers, seeing the war as an opportunity for a change of order in Russia, wished for German victory and therefore surrendered in great masses.[11]

In areas where local frontline army officers understood the need to win the hearts of a local population, there was an almost complete absence of Soviet partisan activity and a high degree of cooperation in the growing and distribution of food. But once the soldiers moved on and rear-echelon officers or civilian administrators took over, the treatment of the people, and consequently their attitude toward the Germans, changed.

It was not only defense of the Soviet Union that kept many Red Army soldiers fighting against the Germans, it was the security troops of the NKVD (later the KGB). Better armed than the regular army soldiers, this communist equivalent of the Nazi SS prowled the territory behind the Red Army front lines, killing would-be deserters, defectors, and those who advanced too slowly to satisfy them.

These same troops roamed the countryside in Soviet-controlled territory and executed countless civilians suspected of participating in the one thing Stalin feared more than the German invasion: an anticommunist uprising that could result in the disintegration of the Red Army in the same way the czar's army crumbled in World War I.

One can only imagine how great Hitler's success in the war against the Soviet Union would have been if the Germans had treated the population there with greater compassion. In his history of Soviet partisan activity during the war, Matthew Cooper envisioned the result had German policy toward the Soviet population been different:

Had the Germans recognized the advantage to them that lay in the political realities behind the facade of the Soviet Union and accordingly treated the peoples of the occupied areas as allies in the fight against Bolshevism, the collapse of the Soviet system might well have been brought about.[12]

7

OPENING THE DOOR FOR ROOSEVELT

It was perhaps the greatest error, and certainly
the single most decisive act, of the
Second World War.

Martin Gilbert

Before the Japanese attack on the U.S. fleet at Pearl Harbor rendered the question academic, the United States had been the most activist and belligerent neutral nation in history.

For almost two years President Franklin Roosevelt goaded and harassed Adolf Hitler. Roosevelt tried to provoke Hitler into an act that would provide the excuse he needed to force the U.S. Congress and population to turn their backs on the noninterventionist position and enter the war against Germany. Hitler did everything possible to avoid any incident that might alter the U.S. public's opposition to active participation in the then exclusively European war.

U.S. public opinion was divided between the interventionist position of the Roosevelt administration and its supporters and the noninterventionists such as Charles Lindbergh.

The average American felt that it was right to send ships and war matériel to aid Great Britain but stopped short of committing U.S. soldiers to fight in Europe. Hitler strove to avoid doing anything to endanger that position.

Adolf Hitler remembered all too well that U.S. direct military intervention was the decisive factor in the outcome of World War I. Helene Hanfstaengel, wife of the German publisher Ernst Hanfstaengel, and a woman who was greatly admired by Hitler for her beauty and intelligence, has testified about Hitler's memory, "The only thing that brought our defeat in 1918 was that America entered the war. . . . that must never happen again."[1]

In many respects the dictator's attitude toward the United States was as confused as his feelings about Great Britain. Partly because of the devastating result of U.S. participation in World War I and partly because he recognized that nation's awesome industrial potential, he feared the United States as a powerful adversary. On the one hand he expressed admiration for the efficient manner in which the United States had isolated and exterminated many of the "red savages" who had inhabited the American West and had not been tamed.[2] Yet he also ridiculed U.S. military power as "one big bluff" and "incapable of conducting war." The United States, Hitler concluded, was "half-Judaized, half-Negrified . . . Americans have the brains of a hen."[3]

While Adolf Hitler and Franklin Roosevelt held opposing political philosophies, the U.S. president did everything he could to involve his country in the war. However, U.S. public opinion kept Roosevelt on a short tether. Throughout 1940 and 1941 the polls "consistently showed that approximately 80 per cent of the American people opposed a declaration of war by the United States. Opposition to Hitler's Germany, sympathy for Britain and China, support for aid short of war, and opposition to a declaration of war—those were the American views."[4]

Hitler did everything he could to avoid changing U.S. public opinion, even when it meant jeopardizing the lives of German sailors. David Irving explains:

Toward the United States Hitler was to display unwonted patience despite extreme provocations for one long year. American citizens fought in the Royal Air Force, and United States warships shadowed Axis merchant ships plying their trade in transatlantic waters. The admiralty in Berlin knew from its radio reconnaissance that the Americans were passing on to the British the information about these blockade runners. In vain Admiral Raeder protested to Hitler about this "glaring proof of the United States' nonneutrality." He asked whether to ignore this was "compatible with the honor of the German Reich." But nothing would alter Hitler's determined refusal to take up the American gauntlet flung down to Germany.[5]

Hitler's determination to keep the United States from entering the war in Europe makes his subsequent declaration of war on the United States his most incongruous decision of the entire war.

The Japanese attack on the U.S. fleet at Pearl Harbor came as a complete surprise to the Nazis. Hitler wanted Japan to attack the Soviet Union, thereby forcing Stalin to divert troops to the east and relieve pressure on the German army.

Several days before the attack on Pearl Harbor, Hitler made a verbal commitment to Japanese Foreign Minister Yosuke Matsuoka, promising to join Japan in any future conflict with the United States. He was unaware that the Japanese fleet was already steaming toward Pearl Harbor, prepared to strike the first blow, and his support was being solicited for a war Japan was initiating with neither his knowledge nor his consent.

Although it can never be known exactly what Hitler was thinking at the time, it is not unreasonable to assume he was entering into what he believed to be a trade-off: Germany's support in a future war between Japan and the United States in exchange for Japan's immediate help with Germany's war against the Soviet Union. While this would appear to be a rational explanation for his actions, it does not explain why he failed to obtain a guarantee of such assistance from Matsuoka. In fact, even in the draft of a treaty guaranteeing German support for Japan, Hitler still made no mention of Japan's support against the Soviet Union.

The Japanese were fearful that Hitler would demand a quid pro quo on the issue and instructed their representative in Berlin, General Hiroshi Oshima, to remain evasive if the Germans pursued it.

If [they] question you about our attitude toward the Soviet, say that we have already clarified our attitude toward the Russians in our statement of last July. Say that by our present moves southward we do not mean to relax our pressure against the Soviet and that if Russia joins hands tighter with England and the United States and resists us with hostilities, we are ready to turn upon her with all our might. However, right now, it is to our advantage to stress the south and for the time being we would prefer to refrain from any direct moves in the north.[6]

Tokyo pressured Oshima to obtain German consent to the treaty without telling him that the fleet which would strike the opening blow in the war with the United States was already at sea. The Japanese were trying to put Hitler into a box. They wanted German support for their war against the United States, but they realized they could not wage a war against Great Britain and the United States successfully if they also had to fight the Soviet Union.

When word reached Hitler at his Wolf's Lair headquarters on December 7, 1941, that Japan had launched a successful attack against the United States, he was elated. Waving the message, he rushed to the military bunker, where he exclaimed to Field Marshal Keitel and General Jodl, "We cannot lose the war. Now we have a partner who has not been defeated in three thousand years."[7]

Later, after he had time to reflect on the consequences of the attack on Pearl Harbor, especially the fact that now Stalin could be assured the Japanese would be engaged elsewhere and not on his own eastern frontiers, thus freeing up even more Asian troops for the war against the German invaders, Hitler was less than jubilant. In fact, he told Martin Bormann that the war with the United States was a "tragedy. It is illogical and devoid of any foundations of reality."[8]

When he returned to Berlin the next day, Hitler was told by Foreign Minister von Ribbentrop that the Japanese ambassador had requested a German declaration of war against the United States. The German foreign minister favored the idea of a new ally against Britain, but not the acquisition of a formidable new enemy. He attempted to dissuade Hitler from declaring war against the United States:

I told him that according to the stipulation of the Three-Power Pact, since Japan had attacked, we would not have to declare war, formally. The Fuehrer thought this matter over quite a while and then he gave me a very clear decision. "If we don't stand on the side of Japan," he said, "the Pact is politically dead. But that is not the main reason. The chief reason is that the United States already is shooting against our ships. They have been a forceful factor in this war and through their actions have already created a situation of war."[9]

Thus, in a wholly unilateral decision, without consulting anyone or soliciting the opinions of his military and naval leaders, Adolf Hitler alone declared war on the most powerful industrial state in the world. The question, then and now, remains Why? Yes, it was true the U.S. navy had for many months been acting as if it was already a belligerent in the war, yet German U-boats continued to sink Allied merchant ships almost daily in the Atlantic despite the help the British received from the Americans.

So, on December 11, 1941, Adolf Hitler addressed the

Reichstag. He attacked Roosevelt as a "warmonger" who was backed by the Jews and millionaires responsible for starting the war. He seized this opportunity to vent the storehouse of anger that had built up in him over the previous three years against Roosevelt, who had ceaselessly attacked Hitler as a "gangster":

I understand only too well that a world-wide distance separates Roosevelt's ideas and my ideas. Roosevelt comes from a rich family and belongs to the class whose path is smoothed in the democracies. I was only the child of a small, poor family and had to fight my way by work and industry. When the Great War came Roosevelt occupied a position where he got to know only its pleasant consequences, enjoyed by those who do business while others bleed. I was only one of those who carried out orders as an ordinary soldier, and naturally returned from the war just as poor as I was in the autumn of 1914. I shared the fate of millions, and Franklin Roosevelt only the fate of the so-called Upper Ten Thousand.[10]

Hitler ended his scathing personal attack on Roosevelt by expelling the U.S. chargé d'affaires, who was handed his passport and told to leave Germany because a state of war now existed between the Reich and the United States.

Reading Hitler's complete, rambling, vitriolic speech, one is struck with the thought that Hitler was not really declaring war against the United States, but against Franklin Roosevelt, who had attacked and insulted him so often. Hitler knew the U.S. public was against becoming involved in the war, and that Roosevelt was considered by many Americans to be a "warmonger" who used every trick he could to drag his country into the war. Perhaps in his twisted way of thinking, Hitler felt he was challenging Roosevelt personally.

For Hitler the advantages of declaring war against the United States outweighed the disadvantages, although it is doubtful he considered the latter at all. Because the declaration was one of those important decisions Hitler reached alone, without conferring with anyone else, we shall never know precisely what went through his mind.

One decided advantage was, as Field Marshal Keitel wrote in his memoirs, that "it certainly brought us some relief from the consequences of America's undeclared state of war with us."[11] The declaration and his personal decision-making process also gave Hitler a brief respite from grappling with an even larger and more immediate problem: the war with the Soviet Union.

Hitler had expected that his blitzkrieg against the Soviet Union would result in a decisive German victory and occupation of all European Russia by the end of 1941. But now, at the beginning of December, he was forced to face the truth: that his armies were bogged down in the Russian heartland, with little hope of advancing any farther until spring. The day after the Japanese attack on Pearl Harbor, Hitler issued his Directive 39. It began with these ominous words: "The severe winter weather which has come surprisingly early in the East, and the consequent difficulties in bringing up supplies, compel us to abandon immediately all major offensive operations and to go over to the defensive."[12]

The declaration of war against the United States thus provided Hitler momentary relief from the failure of his plans for the conquest of European Russia. But the situation in the Soviet Union continued to worsen, and except for the German navy, which was now free to attack U.S. ships, the declaration and the United States were all but forgotten. Everyone in Germany expected the Americans to concentrate on fighting against the enemy in the Pacific that had physically attacked them and had so badly damaged their navy and national pride. Most Americans expected the same.

President Roosevelt did not subscribe to that brand of thinking. He agreed with Winston Churchill that the Japanese threat in Asia could be dealt with later. The main enemy was the Axis powers in Europe, and the European war would take precedence over the Pacific war.

While the members of the Reichstag may have cheered Hitler's declaration of war, not all Germans did. John Toland reported that the German Foreign Office saw it as a "colossal mistake."

In addition to the obvious reasons it neatly solved another of Roosevelt's domestic problems. The President would not have to declare war on Germany and risk opposition from a substantial segment of the citizenry. American national unity, so unexpectedly won by the surprise attack at Pearl Harbor, would remain intact.[13]

It is important to remember that Americans were still largely opposed to sending troops to fight in Europe. The Japanese had attacked the United States, and the United States would retaliate, but that had nothing to do with Europe. If Hitler had not declared war on the United States, Roosevelt would have had no choice but to concentrate his armed forces against Japan, as his army and navy leaders wanted.

Given the German belief that the United States would focus its efforts against Japan first, and Hitler's hope that Japan would go to war against the Soviet Union if he declared war on the United States, Hitler's decision to make the United States an active opponent makes sense. But, as far as the former was concerned, Roosevelt's continued hatred for Hitler should have made the German leader understand that the U.S. president was determined to bring him down, even at the expense of allowing the Japanese carte blanche in the Pacific for several years.

Had he been thinking clearly, Hitler should have realized that for most Americans war with Japan did not necessarily mean war with Germany. Hitler lacked any real knowledge about the United States and how a democracy worked. Therefore he never quite understood his own influence on

U.S. affairs. He assumed the noninterventionists in the United States would continue to oppose war, even after the country was attacked. He misread them as pacifists when they were really isolationists opposed to sending troops to fight in Europe, but not to defending their own country.

If Hitler's war declaration was made to appease an important ally, then he failed to understand the significance of courting Japan as his ally. He never requested that the Japanese trade a German war against the United States for active Japanese support in the war against the Soviet Union. By failing to demand such a quid pro quo, he jettisoned his chances for a possible Japanese attack against the Soviet Union, which would have forced Stalin into the dreaded military dilemma of a two-front war. Japan's only possible value to Germany was as a direct partner against Moscow, yet Hitler never insisted the Japanese join him, and they never did. The only thing to which the Japanese agreed was a joint pledge by Japan, Germany, and Italy not to seek or conclude a separate peace. Hitler maintained such a benevolent attitude toward the Japanese that he was not even angered that they had not told him of their plans to attack the United States.

If Hitler saw U.S. intervention in the European conflict as inevitable, and judged that intervention would result, as it did in World War I, in Germany's defeat even after her largest opponent, Russia, was out of the war, then he had some justification for expecting that the Japanese attack could prolong the interval before that intervention. But even that was clutching at a straw in the wind.

Hitler's swift declaration of war against the United States defies all logic. A U.S. State Department team sent to Germany immediately after the war sought the answer to why Hitler made this incomprehensible blunder. They found no answer to what they considered the "most baffling question in the whole Nazi story."

What would have happened if Hitler had not brought the

United States into the war in Europe? The influence on the war in the Soviet Union would likely have been negligible. U.S. involvement had little immediate impact on the war in Europe for some time, except for an increase in U.S. shipments of oil and other war matériel to Britain.

Without Hitler's brash action President Roosevelt would have been constrained to concentrate U.S. military action against Japan. Great pressure would have been brought on him to reduce aid to the British and Soviets, and to divert that same matériel to U.S. forces fighting in the Pacific. Without Hitler's declaration the United States would have looked west to Japan, and not east toward Europe, for its main theater of operations. The American people eagerly sought revenge for Japan's "sneak attack." Hitler's declaration of war siphoned some of their anger away from Japan and directed it at Germany.

While the immediate result of signing the declaration of war against the United States was minimal, the long-term effect for Adolf Hitler was the signing of his own death warrant. Had he not made this "colossal mistake," Hitler could have avoided U.S. involvement in the war in Europe for perhaps as long as two or three years. During that time the Germans could have defeated or come to satisfactory terms with Stalin, kept the Americans out of the war in Africa, prevented the Allied invasion of Italy, and given Germany's scientists and technicians the time they required to develop and build the technologically advanced weapons Germany so desperately needed three years later.

8

HITLER SLEPT LATE

"Has the Fuehrer been awakened?" I asked.
"No, he receives the news after he has
eaten his breakfast."
Albert Speer

By early spring of 1944, the buildup of U.S. troops in south-west England had swollen to mammoth proportions in prep-aration for the invasion of Europe. By D-Day 1.5 million GIs would be marshaled on English soil. There were so many U.S. soldiers quartered in southern England that the British laughingly referred to that section of their country as "occu-pied England."

In London, U.S. General Dwight D. Eisenhower, supreme commander of all Allied forces in Europe, set June 5 as the date for the planned landings on the beaches of Normandy, in northern France. Operation Point-blank, an Anglo-Amer-ican campaign that targeted the key German industrial areas of the Rhur and the Saar for around-the-clock bombing, clearly established that the Allies now controlled the skies over Europe.

By mid May southern England was completely isolated from the rest of the world. Civilian traffic was halted, telephone and mail services were curtailed, and final rehearsals for the D-Day landings were conducted along the beaches. U.S. and British fighter pilots intensified their operations against the Luftwaffe to solidify Allied air superiority over the landing sites.

On June 4 the weather worsened dramatically. Many of the invasion ships already at sea were badly buffeted, causing widespread seasickness among the invasion troops. At 9:45 on the evening of June 4, the severe weather forced Eisenhower to postpone the invasion. As weathermen pored over their data, D-Day was rescheduled for dawn on June 6.

Thousands of invasion craft left their moorings and proceeded toward their rendezvous points. In the early evening of June 5, Eisenhower personally visited the paratroopers of the U.S. 82nd and 101st Airborne Divisions, assigned to drop behind the German lines hours before the scheduled landings.

Just before dawn on June 6, at a rendezvous spot called Piccadilly Circus, Operation Overlord, the code name for the invasion, began. An invasion armada numbering 6,000 ships assembled for the assault on the Normandy beachhead. Four and a half hours earlier 20,000 paratroopers of the 82nd and 101st Airborne had jumped into the darkness of the French countryside around Ste. Mère Eglise. The infantrymen of the British 6th Airborne Division landed in gliders farther east, around the French village of Benouville, six miles north of Caen, an important communications center.

Within hours of this silent invasion, large Allied naval guns opened fire on the German defenses along 60 miles of the Normandy coast. Troop-carrying ships dropped their assault barges over the side, and U.S. and British troops poured into them. Tens of thousands of anxious men stood mostly in silence as they were ferried across the choppy water to their appointment with Hitler's defenders and their private destinies. Allied bombers, with virtual control of the air, bombed coastal defenses mercilessly to soften them for the landing forces. Farther inland, Allied fighters strafed every German target they could find.

As the assault troops neared the beaches, the guns of Hitler's vaunted Atlantic Wall opened fire. On the western flank of the invasion, the U.S. Seventh Corps, under the command of General J. L. Collins, would land at Utah Beach, located at the base of the Cotentin Peninsula. Its immediate objective was to establish a beachhead between La Madeleine and Varreville and join with the airborne units at Ste. Mère Eglise, then move west and north to cut off the peninsula and capture the port of Cherbourg.

The first wave of 600 men of the U.S. Fourth Infantry Division assaulted the beach aboard 20 boats. Engineers cleared the mines and obstacles that formed the first line of defense at the water's edge. Resistance and casualties were surprisingly light. Within one hour the beach had been secured, and the men pressed inland for their rendezvous with the paratroopers.

East of Utah Beach was Omaha Beach, a five-mile stretch of shoreline with a backdrop of gently rising bluffs. The U.S. Fifth Corps, led by the First Division, was ordered to establish a beachhead, capture the coastal towns, and reach the road running from Bayeux to Caen by nightfall.

In this sector, German mortar and machine-gun fire was devastating. The soldiers wading ashore through chest-high water suffered heavy casualties. German resistance was fierce, and the beach quickly became littered with equipment that was wrecked as soon as it came ashore. Most of the amphibious tanks sent in with the first wave were sunk. Despite the terrible cost, the beachhead was finally secured.

Farther east, the British Second Army, under General Miles C. Dempsey, struggled through three-foot waves toward its objectives. The 50th Division of the British 30th Corps landed at Gold Beach, between the towns of La Rivière and La Hamel. The Canadian Third Division of the British First Corps assaulted Juno Beach, between Courselles and Bernières. The British Third Division fought its way ashore between Lion Sur Mer and Ouistreham, on a beach code-named Sword.

Within an hour of landing, elements of the British 50th Division were more than a mile inland and headed toward Bayeux. At Juno the Canadians moved swiftly and decisively against withering machine-gun fire from the defenders, and fought their way into their coastal village targets.

At Sword Beach the British Third Division was frozen on the beach, held down by heavy artillery fire from a ridge commanding the coast. The setback was temporary, however, and the Third Division regrouped and pushed hard against the defenders until they were overrun.

Although the German defenses were strong and active, they failed to offer the level of resistance expected by the Allied planners. A major reason for this became clear when the invaders rounded up masses of German prisoners who could not speak German. The Allied commanders were shocked to learn that a large portion of the troops defending Hitler's Fortress Europe were not Germans but less reliable troops from the East, including thousands of former Soviet POWs who, while enthusiastic about fighting the Red Army, were less than eager to fight the British and Americans.

Much of the success of the D-Day invasion of Normandy was due to Adolf Hitler's poor planning and flawed decisions. He alone was responsible for the condition and quality of the troops who were assigned the task of throwing back the massive Allied invasion of Europe that everyone in German-occupied Europe knew was coming.

As pointed out earlier, Hitler had the misconception that he could create fighting units out of thin air. An obsession with numbers, especially numbers of his divisions, deluded

him into thinking that the extra divisions he created by transferring a few old men into a newly designated unit, and thus
pinning another divisional symbol on his operational maps,
would have a corresponding positive influence in the field. It
was such phantom divisions that were to defend the Third
Reich from the enemy forces flooding across the English
Channel.

Lieutenant General Bodo Zimmerman, chief operations
officer to Field Marshal von Rundstedt, described the organizational and tactical dispositions of the German army in the
West as "a mere patchwork":

Commanders, troops and equipment became, quite frankly, sec-
ond-rate. From 1943 on, the basis of the Western Army consisted
of over-age men armed with over-age weapons. Neither the one
nor the other were a match, even physically, for the demands of the
coming heavy invasion battle.[1]

Even though he was nominally the commander in chief in
the West, von Rundstedt had no direct control over the antiaircraft units and parachute troops. These organizations
were controlled by Göring's Luftwaffe. The SS divisions
stationed throughout occupied France reported to Reich-
führer Himmler. This arrangement greatly hampered von
Runstedt's ability to maneuver fighting units effectively in
the stress of the invasion battles, when mobility was para-
mount. The result was that von Rundstedt was commander
of an area vital to Germany's defense which was so badly
fragmented that effective control was impossible.

Von Rundstedt complained bitterly to Hitler about this
fragmentation. His protests were fruitless, since Hitler himself had created the dilemma. Fear of allowing any army
commander to acquire sufficient power over the movement
of troops that might be used against him compelled Hitler to
withhold from every army commander the power to defeat
the enemy. Through his puppets in the OKW, Hitler domi-

nated every detail of the preparations for the defense of the French coast. "In all major decisions—for instance, if he wanted to move a division—he [von Rundstedt] had to consult OKW."[2]

Hitler further decimated his already fragmented and badly diluted defense forces, which consisted largely of old men and recuperating walking wounded staffing undermanned shadow divisions, by transferring 20 of his best-trained and -equipped battalions to the slaughterhouse the Soviet campaign had become. In their place came the "volunteers" from the POW camps, many of them former Soviet soldiers who had volunteered to fight against the Red Army out of conviction but had little stomach to fight the Western Allies. Others had volunteered for anything that would take them out of the dreadful conditions of the camps that were run by the SS.

In all, some 60,000 of these "Eastern volunteers" were assigned to defend western Europe. Aside from their lack of fervor, the mixture of so many non-German tongues among the troops created great organizational difficulties, ranging from issuing combat orders to the distribution of pay. One example of this was that pay books had to be issued in eight different languages.

Hitler further exacerbated the situation in the West by sending Field Marshal Erwin Rommel to inspect the "Atlantic Wall." Although the hero of the North African campaign was ostensibly under the command of von Rundstedt, the old field marshal was not permitted to give Rommel a direct order. Rommel found the partially built fortifications to be a "figment" of Hitler's imagination. He called it an "enormous bluff."[3]

The "Atlantic Wall" was a great monument to the military bungling and stupidity of Adolf Hitler. At a time when such supplies were desperately needed elsewhere, the construction of these fixed fortifications required, in just two years, 17.3 million cubic yards of concrete and 1.2 million metric tons of iron. The iron could have been put to much better use by the armament factories.[4] Besides this waste of raw materials, "Most of the weapons for the Atlantic Wall, down to the mines and even barbed wire, were taken from the old West Wall along the Franco-German frontier."[5]

It is difficult to justify the expenditure of so much effort on fixed fortifications by the man who had demonstrated the futility of such outdated relics of earlier wars when he invaded France in 1940. The Allied invasion of Normandy skirted Hitler's forts almost as easily as the German army had bypassed the Maginot Line four years earlier.

Although von Rundstedt and Rommel apparently respected each other's abilities, the two men could not agree on how the defense against the inevitable invasion should be prepared. Rommel thought the only chance of a successful defense was to fight the invasion on the beaches, denying Allied troops a foothold anywhere. Von Rundstedt saw it differently. He opted for permitting the Allies to gain a beachhead from which they could not easily escape. He proposed to mass the panzers in reserve locations behind the invasion front so they could launch a quick, decisive counterattack against the invaders once the Germans knew the disposition of all enemy forces. The panzers would, as von Rundstedt saw it, drive the invading army into the sea. Obviously he sought to re-create the conditions at Dunkirk four years earlier, when the British army had faced annihilation. Because he controlled all troop movements and made all decisions, it was up to Hitler to decide which defense to implement.

In his typical style, Hitler refused to support either plan. Instead he gave each man a little of what he wanted. The result was that neither strategy could succeed because the available forces were spread too thin. "Hitler arbitrated and arranged a compromise, telling Rommel to defeat the landings on the beaches with the help of some armored forces held nearby and let von Rundstedt retain a diluted central reserve for the main punch if the enemy was not checked on the shoreline."[6]

It is clear from the personal history of these two professional soldiers that if Hitler, who obviously was too much of
an amateur in these matters to make a firm decision, had decided on either defense strategy, or had developed one of his
own, both men would have worked to the best of their ability
to see that the defense succeeded.

When the U.S. army's official history of the war was written, the disagreement over defense strategy between the
German field marshals received special attention because
Hitler's resolution practically assured failure: "In summary,
the conflict between Rommel's and [von] Rundstedt's theories of defense was never resolved definitely in favor of one or
the other and led to compromise troop dispositions which on
D-Day were not suitable for the practice of either theory."[7]

The opposing defense strategies of von Rundstedt and
Rommel, the latter having been given command of Army
Group B, which covered the invasion front under von
Rundstedt, is a debate that will never be resolved. For half a
century military historians and strategists, both armchair
and professional, have come down about equally for one side
or the other.

Because of Rommel's reputation among his former enemies, many Western observers lean toward his defense,
pointing out the weakness in von Rundstedt's reliance on
massed panzer units. Since the Allied air forces had virtual
supremacy in the air over western Europe, the German ability to mass and quickly move large numbers of tanks was extremely limited.

On the other hand, von Rundstedt saw in Rommel's shoreline defense a weakness that the German army had exhibited
in its defense against Allied landings in Sicily and Italy. Despite the courage of the defenders, the combination of air
superiority and the naval guns of the great Allied warships
was decisive in hammering the Germans into defeat. Von
Rundstedt expected the impending invasion to be gigantic
and violent. He felt it foolish to defend the beaches against

the bombardment of naval guns against which the Germans could not retaliate. Land-based artillery would not reach the ships, and the Luftwaffe could be practically discounted for the rest of the war, so there would be no German bombs dropped on the ships. The specter of German soldiers hiding in the concrete bunkers while the Allied ships fired tons of shells at them seemed to him an inappropriate defense.

Whichever man was right, Hitler saw to it that neither had enough troops or matériel from what was available to effectively conduct the defense he proposed. Hitler's inability to make a decisive choice in favor of one defense over another ensured that the Allies would succeed.

When the invasion actually began with the assaults by parachute and glider forces, von Rundstedt took immediate action. One of his first orders was the mobilization of two powerful panzer divisions that were held in reserve by Hitler through the OKW. These were the Panzer Lehr Division, stationed southwest of Paris, and the 12th SS Hitlerjugend Panzer Division, stationed in western France. Von Rundstedt ordered both divisions to speed toward Caen, under command of Rommel's Army Group B. Rommel was not at his headquarters at the time.

Three hours later, at 6 A.M., von Rundstedt received a call confirming what he expected: An Allied landing was taking place between the Orne and Vire rivers and farther north. The field marshal felt vindicated for having ordered the OKW panzer reserve divisions into action. He knew the Allies would not commit valuable crack parachute and glider troops on the Continent and not immediately support them with an invasion. To do otherwise would leave these troops vulnerable to decimation by the enemy.

Unfortunately, a few minutes after receiving the call confirming the invasion, von Rundstedt received another call. This one was from OKW. The field marshal was harshly reprimanded, in no uncertain terms, for having assumed command of the two OKW panzer divisions without prior approval from Hitler. He was told the two divisions had been ordered to halt their advance and that they would remain stopped until Hitler personally ordered them to move.

Field Marshal von Rundstedt's operations officer describes what happened next.

Throughout the morning and early afternoon I, the Chief of Staff, General Blumentritt, and Rundstedt himself repeatedly telephoned the OKW, in order to find out what Hitler had decided in the matter of these two divisions. Apparently he was asleep, and no one dared wake him. It was not until his usual conference, between three and four o'clock that afternoon, that Hitler decided to allow the commitment of the divisions. They were immediately ordered to resume their advance.

But by then it was too late. During the morning, and until 1100 hours, a hazy fog had covered Normandy. This would have provided the divisions with some protection from air attack and have permitted rapid movement. Now the haze had dissipated, and the whole area through which the divisions must march was being intensively patrolled by the Allied air forces. No road movement by day was possible in view of this air umbrella, which reached from Normandy to the Paris area.[8]

When the two panzer divisions resumed their advance, they came under intense attack by Allied fighters and bombers, suffering heavy casualties in both men and tanks long before they were able to reach the actual battleground.

Albert Speer, minister of armaments, gives a description of what he found at Hitler's headquarters on the morning of the D-Day invasion.

On June 6, I was at the Berghof about ten o'clock in the morning when one of Hitler's military adjutants told me that the invasion had begun early that morning.

"Has the Fuehrer been awakened?" I asked.

He shook his head. "No, he receives the news after he has eaten breakfast."[9]

Hitler frequently expressed fear of a two-front war. He was of course referring to an Allied invasion of France, but the Normandy invasion actually opened Germany's third front. On the second front, Italy, the Allies were steadily pushing back the German army.

Hitler knew the invasion was coming. He was not sure when or exactly where, but there had been so much intelligence that it was imminent that it is incredible to think Hitler continued his lifelong habit of sleeping late each morning. Even more incredible are his actions on D-Day after he learned the long-feared invasion was finally under way. Hard to believe but nevertheless historically true, the man who slept late each morning, and casually pursued his normal routine on the day of the most massive invasion in history, was the same man who three months earlier, on March 18, 1944, had told a meeting of all the generals in the west at Berchtesgarten that "the whole outcome of the war depends on each man fighting in the west, and that means the fate of the Reich itself."[10]

His first tactical error was to assume, without any evidence, that the Normandy invasion was a feint. Ironically, the invasion took place at the precise location he himself had originally predicted it would. In the interim he had convinced himself the invasion's first objective would be the launch sites of the V-bombs that were being sent against English cities. He had convinced himself these rockets were taking a terrible toll on the British population and morale. Assuming this to be true, then the area around Calais would presumably be the main objective of the invasion. It was typical of Hitler to apply convoluted logic to arrive at a conclusion that satisfied him, then treat that conclusion as if it were indisputable fact. He failed to understand that the objective of a large seaborne invasion is to gain a solid foothold through which the invaders can channel the mass of men and matériel needed to defeat the defenders. The V-bomb launch pads were only one of a long list of important targets.

After breakfast and a briefing on the status of the invasion, Hitler took a leisurely one-hour drive. His destination was Klessheim Castle, where he was to entertain the prime minister of Hungary, General Dome Sztojay. The reception for the state visit was held in the castle that had once belonged to the prince-archbishop of Salzburg, a setting of breathtaking beauty. Hitler liked impressing his allies.

At his customary noon military briefing, during which the positions of British and U.S. forces were shown on a map of France, Hitler chuckled, as if they were headed into some great trap that only he knew about. During the reception for Sztojay, Hitler and his flunkies lied about everything connected with the war, including arms production statistics, the strength of German forces, and their recent advances. In reality there were no German advances. Hitler's armies were falling back everywhere they confronted an enemy. He capped the visit with an announcement that Germany had developed a secret weapon which would reduce English cities to ashes.[11]

As German forces fought a life-and-death struggle with the invading Allies, Hitler acted as if nothing unusual had happened. His only contribution to the war effort in France was to allow the panzer units that von Rundstedt had ordered to advance to resume their advance. Even that was too little, too late. The successful invasion signaled the beginning of the end for Nazi Germany. Hitler knew it, and he took no concrete action to stop it.

9

JEWISH SCIENCE AND
MIRACLE WEAPONS

> If the dismissal of Jewish scientists means the
> annihilation of German science, then we shall
> have to do without science for a few years.
> Adolf Hitler

Ever since 1945 historians and military strategists have spec-
ulated on what might have happened if the Nazis had developed an atomic bomb. The real question is Why didn't the
Nazis develop an atomic bomb? The answer lies squarely
with Adolf Hitler.

Because of Hitler's vehement anti-Semitism many key
scientists who were capable of developing the bomb were
murdered or driven out of Germany. Those scientists who remained were hamstrung by Hitler's conviction that nuclear
physics was a "Jewish science." They also labored against interference from incompetent Nazi leaders who hampered
the research and development of virtually every new weapons project. The worst offenders were Göring and Himmler,

who sought scientific advancement as a means for personal enrichment and increased personal power.

Despite the efforts of such ranking advisers as Albert Speer to solicit support for an atomic bomb project, Hitler lacked the imagination and interest to back them. Without his full support no project could expect to reach the magnitude required for meaningful results.

Aside from the loss of many of the leading scientists in nuclear research, there were two critical reasons Nazi Germany failed to develop an atomic bomb, even while its Asian ally was building several small test models. As Albert Speer pointed out, the first of these was that a device as powerful as the atomic bomb "obviously strained [Hitler's] intellectual capacity."[1]

It seemed to Speer that Hitler could not grasp the concepts of nuclear physics and therefore ignored its possibilities. It was not the first time, nor would it be the last, that Hitler ignored or ridiculed something of profound importance because he failed to understand it. What would have happened if the Nazis had built an atomic bomb? Speer, who is universally accepted as an authority on Hitler's predilection in such a situation, stated categorically: "I am sure that Hitler would not have hesitated for a moment to employ atomic bombs against England."[2]

The second compelling reason atomic research never succeeded in Nazi Germany was the manner in which Hitler fragmented everything in his government, including scientific research and development programs. There were never any clear lines of responsibility making people accountable for their lack of performance. The level of incompetence of many Nazi scientists, with a few notable exceptions, was such that they welcomed the opportunity the decentralized, fragmented bureaucracy gave them to shift the blame for failures to others.

The fragmented fabric of Hitler's scientific community created an atmosphere of mistrust and a truly unhealthy competition among various groups of researchers for the limited resources available. Projects for the development of high-tech weapons were conducted by many major departments of the German government. These included the security services of the SS and even such unlikely agencies as the post office.

The dismal result of this hodgepodge was described by General Walter Dornberger, head of the rocket research center at Peenemunde:

New [research] organizations were springing up like mushrooms after rain alongside the old and tried ones and inflating themselves furiously. In most cases there was overlapping if not actual duplication. All the departmental bosses, out of suspicion, lust for power or sheer obstinacy, then jealously fought for independence. Occasionally a new organization with few but able men in it had the drive to score certain initial success. This, it alleged, justified its existence and even entitled it to expand. In no time it grew just as cumbersome and hidebound as the predecessors or competitors which it claimed had been failures.[3]

One area that commanded Hitler's enthusiastic interest, especially when it became clear that Germany faced defeat unless heroic measures were taken, was the development of what Hitler called "miracle weapons." Yet throughout the war, and especially in the decisive two years before Germany's fall, Hitler constantly threw obstacles in the way of the development of technologically advanced weapons.

Among Germany's "miracle weapons" was a group of jet aircraft that included fighter planes and bombers. The most promising of these, built by Messerschmitt, was called the ME 262. A preserved example of this jet fighter is displayed at the Air and Space Museum in Washington, DC. Speer called the ME 262 "the most valuable of our 'secret weapons.'"[4]

Germany's leading ace, General of Fighters Adolf Galland, flew an ME 262 on May 22, 1943. Impressed by the capabilities of the jet that felt "as though an angel's pushing," the ace assured the Luftwaffe leaders, "The aircraft could be our biggest chance, it could guarantee us an unimaginable lead over the enemy if he adheres to the piston engine." The new jet, he told everyone, "will give us such a lead that even a few would make an enormous difference to us."[5]

Although it was only one of several jet fighters that were developed and actually flight-tested, many of Germany's fighter aces singled out the ME 262 as the ultimate weapon they needed to rid the sky of U.S. bombers. With the ability to fly at speeds exceeding the fastest Allied fighters by at least 150 miles per hour, the ME 262 was capable of eluding Allied fighter escorts and sweeping into formations of enemy bombers, just as, earlier in the war, German U-boats swept past escorting warships to bring death and destruction to convoys.

The first ME 262 was flown in July 1942. Because of bureaucratic bungling and Hitler's interference, the jet failed to enter combat service until the fall of 1944. By this time it was too late to change the outcome of the war. If it had participated in the defense of Germany against the massive bomber raids during the year or more it should have been operational, it might have regained control of the skies from the Allies. Since control of the skies made victory on the ground possible, the outcome of the war might have been altered without the Allies' overwhelming air superiority.

The design work and subsequent production of the ME 262 were plagued with infighting among the powerful personalities involved, particularly Field Marshal Milch and Professor Willy Messerschmitt, who despised each other. Although Milch was in charge of production for the Luftwaffe, and Messerschmitt's company was a prime Luftwaffe contractor, they seemed more often to be working at odds, right up to the end of the war and even afterward, each blaming the other for the failure to build a fleet of ME 262s when it might have mattered. But the crucial obstacle to the production of this fighter was Adolf Hitler.

Hitler scorned the development of fighters, which he identified as defensive weapons. He persisted in fighting an offensive war even when enemy forces were poised to attack Germany itself and the Allies controlled the airspace over Germany, delivering daily destruction to strategic German targets. Hitler still harbored the hope that by attacking British cities, and possibly even New York, he could break the will of the Allied population and bring the war to a halt. Again he proved his blindness to the reality of the crisis in his own country. The Allied bombing of Germany cities did not break the morale of the German civilian population; instead it served to strengthen their resolve to fight back. Had Hitler been successful in bringing the war back to British cities in late 1944 and early 1945, it would have had a similar effect on the British population.

Mistrustful of the new type of aircraft, Hitler abruptly ordered a halt to preparations for its mass production in September 1943. By the following January he changed his mind. He ordered that it be produced in large numbers, but as a bomber rather than a fighter. Despite the efforts of air force specialists to convince him of the value of the ME 262 as a fighter, Hitler obstinately refused to relent. He ordered all weapons and armor removed and their weight replaced with bombs. The jets moved so fast, Hitler reasoned, that they did not require weapons to defend themselves. He then contradicted his own philosophy and ordered that the ME 262's top speed be reduced.

On reflection, it is ludicrous that Hitler even dreamed that this tiny plane with a bomb capacity of, at most, 1,000 pounds could have any appreciable effect on the war when U.S. Flying Fortresses were dropping thousands of tons of bombs on German cities every day. "As fighter planes," Speer wrote, "each one of the jet aircraft would have been able, because of its superior performance, to shoot down several of the four-motored American bombers."[6]

Hitler soon changed his mind about the ME 262. Still opposed to its use as a fighter to defend against Allied bomber attacks, he was now thinking about the expected Allied invasion:

With every month the probability grows that we'll get at least one squadron of jet planes. The vital thing is to rain bombs down on the enemy the moment they invade. Even if there's only one plane up, they'll have to take cover and they'll lose hour after hour! Within half a day we'll be bringing up our reserves. Even if they're pinned down on the beach only six or eight hours, you can figure what that'll mean for them.[7]

This comment typifies Hitler's lack of understanding of air warfare. A squadron of jets, especially undefended bombers—much less one such aircraft—would have had little if any effect on the success of the Allied invasion at Normandy. The success of the invasion was due largely to the Allies' domination of the air over the invasion site and most of northern France. Reserve units of panzers and infantry were subjected to devastating attacks from Allied bombers and fighters that prevented them from moving during daylight hours. This air superiority would have easily destroyed Hitler's figmentary jet bombers before they could reach the invasion beaches.

There is considerable doubt that even the jet fighters could have been much help during the invasion, unless they had been produced in sufficiently large numbers. The value of the jets was completely misunderstood by Hitler. He saw them as a means to repair his damaged ego by throwing a few relatively ineffectual bombs at British cities in retaliation for the massive bombing raids the British and Americans were conducting against German cities. When he progressed beyond that idea he fantasized that these new fast bombers could almost single-handedly stop what he knew would be an enormous invasion force.

The real value of these planes was as a defensive weapon that could be used against the fleets of U.S. bombers over Germany. By raising the cost of the bomber raids to intolerable levels, the Luftwaffe pilots expected to wrest control of the air from the enemy. Blinded to this possibility, and refusing to listen to the experts, Hitler lost the only possible chance he had to stop the bombing that was destroying not only his cities but also the factories that were producing the weapons which enabled him to continue the war.

As the war turned decisively against Germany on all fronts, Hitler continually referred to the "miracle weapons" that would save Germany and destroy her enemies. Many Germans believed him, largely because they knew the unconditional surrender demands of the Allies, and the leaked secret Morgenthau Plan developed by Roosevelt's secretary of the Treasury, would destroy whatever remained of German civilization. The idea of "miracle weapons" gave them hope that things would not turn out so badly after all. It is likely that few in Germany, other than blind Hitler followers, believed a German victory was possible, but many hoped for a negotiated settlement. Ironically, the more Hitler spoke of his "miracle weapons," the more he interfered with their development.

Albert Speer reports that the jet aircraft was not the only advanced weapon Germany was developing:

The jet plane was not the only effective weapon that could have been slated for mass production in 1944. We possessed a remote-controlled flying bomb, a rocket plane that was even faster than the jet plane, a rocket missile that homed on an enemy plane by tracking the heat rays from its motors, and a torpedo that reacted to sound and could thus pursue and hit a ship fleeing in a zig-zag course. Development of a ground-to-air missile had been completed.[8]

Speer explains Hitler's blunders in the development and use
of these advanced weapons:

Once again it was Hitler who, in spite of all the tactical mistakes of
the Allies, ordained those very moves which helped the enemy air
offensive in 1944 achieve its success. After postponing the development of the jet fighter and later converting it into a light bomber,
Hitler now decided to use our big new rockets to retaliate against
England.[9]

Beginning in the summer of 1943, an inordinate amount of
industrial capacity was devoted to the big rockets that became known as the V-2. As with virtually every other
weapon he liked, Hitler ordered the production of more than
Germany was capable of building: 900 each month. This was
another example of Hitler's doctrine that his will and his orders made everything possible. If he ordered 900 built each
month, then he did not have to worry about how that would
be accomplished; he simply believed it would.

The whole idea was absurd. The fleets of enemy bombers in 1944
were dropping an average of three thousand tons of bombs a day
over a span of several months. And Hitler wanted to retaliate with
thirty rockets that would have carried twenty-four tons of explosives to England daily. That was equivalent to the bomb load of
only twelve Flying Fortresses.[10]

As 1944 neared a close, even Hitler realized the war was
lost. In desperation he ordered the construction of a "miracle
fighter." The result was a "Jumbo 004 engine mounted above
the fuselage of a light wooden-and-metal fighter airframe (a
configuration quite like that of the V-1 in many ways) and it
was ordered by Hitler from the Heinkel works on the 8th of
September 1944."[11]
    A demonstration of the plane reportedly took place on De-
cember 10, 1944, for the benefit of high-ranking Nazi and

Luftwaffe officials. The right wing fell off and the plane crashed, killing the pilot. The glue used to hold the wooden parts together was quickly blamed, and production was ordered to go ahead. This wooden airplane was designed to serve as a suicide weapon for young men who would ram them into enemy bombers much like the Japanese kamikazes.

Hitler's habitual interference with the development of realistic advanced weapons resulted in this abortive attempt by a nation responsible for so many technological advances. The Germans were reduced to placing their hope on a wooden airplane. Historian Ronald Lewin wrote, "No form of excuse can relieve Hitler of responsibility for the failure of the Luftwaffe to produce an efficient second generation of aircraft. The damage flowed from his own choice."[12]

10

"MAKE PEACE, YOU FOOLS"

It is not necessary to worry about what the
German people will need for elemental survival.

Adolf Hitler

As certain victory dissolved into inevitable defeat and the
German war machine began to fall apart, Adolf Hitler lost all
sense of reality. As early as June 17, 1944, Field Marshal
Erwin Rommel tried to convince Hitler the war was lost.
Meeting in a previously unused Führerbunker near the
French village of Margival, Rommel summed up the war situation for Hitler. He predicted the Allies would soon break
through the German front in Normandy, and nothing could
stop them from advancing into Germany. The Russians,
Rommel pointed out, were advancing from the east, and a
third Allied army was moving north through Italy. The time
had come, he told a stunned Hitler, to end the war. Shaking
with anger, Hitler shrieked at Rommel, "It is not your privi-
lege to worry about the future course of the war!"[1]
Two weeks later Field Marshal Keitel called Field Marshal

von Rundstedt and listened glumly as the commander of the West reported the hopelessness of the situation. The OKW chief moaned, "What shall we do? What shall we do?" Von Rundstedt's reply was terse and to the point: "Make peace, you fools. What else can you do?"[2]

There would be no peacemaking for Hitler. Even when Berlin was surrounded by Soviet troops moving steadily toward the center of the city, Hitler held fast. Until his death he continued to predict the alliance between the Soviet Union and the Western democracies would collapse. As evidence he was right, he grasped at every trifling indication there might be a disagreement between the Allies. History has since proved he was correct, and the alliance did fall apart, but he did not live to see it happen.

In the end Hitler's madness was directed against the German people. He took measures designed to ensure they would not survive his death. His feelings toward the German population were revealed in the following comment he made to Albert Speer.

If the war is lost, the people will be lost also. It is not necessary to worry about what the German people will need for elemental survival. On the contrary, it is best for us to destroy even these things. For the nation has proved to be the weaker, and the future belongs solely to the stronger eastern nation. In any case only those who are inferior will remain after this struggle, for the good have already been killed.[3]

As he had done throughout his career, Hitler sought to indict others for his own failures. Now he blamed the German people as not worthy of him as their leader. On March 8, 1945, the day after U.S. troops secured a bridgehead across the Rhine, Hitler's high command issued orders for the execution of German soldiers who were surrendering without being wounded or had deserted their units. They were to "be shot at once." In one incident four officers were summarily executed for allowing the Americans to capture the Rhine bridge at Remagen before they could blow it up.

On March 20, Hitler issued his "scorched earth" order, believing it would spell the end of the Third Reich and doom for the German people. It was his response to the realization that the Allies were poised to cross the Rhine en masse and occupy the German heartland, while the Russians were swiftly advancing west from their positions in East Prussia, Silesia, and Hungary. Hitler ordered:

All military transport, and communication facilities, industrial establishments and supply depots, as well as anything else of value within Reich territory, which could in any way be used by the enemy immediately or within the foreseeable future for the prosecution of the war, will be destroyed.[4]

Determined that the German people should answer for their failure to sustain his dream of a Thousand Year Reich, the Führer was prepared to bring about their total destruction.

One of Hitler's final and most ludicrous military blunders was to appoint Heinrich Himmler, the chief Nazi executioner, as commander of Army Group Vistula, defending the northern approaches to Berlin. Himmler had no knowledge of military strategy and immediately surrounded himself with a staff of loyal SS men who were equally inexperienced. General Heinz Guderian, the panzer commander who was serving as Hitler's last chief of the army general staff, "argued and pleaded against the appalling and preposterous appointment."[5]

Himmler proved to be an even more inept military commander than Hitler. The problem was that the SS leader spent most of his time seeking out and executing scapegoats to blame for his own failures. He was so afraid of being killed that he spent almost the entire time as military commander hiding in a railroad tunnel or cowering in a sanatorium.

Almost as if to ensure that the dreaded Soviets would be

first to enter and rape Berlin, Propaganda Minister Joseph Goebbels "fed tidbits of information about the mythical fortress [the Alpine or National Redoubt] system to the Allied and neutral press."[6] In January 1945, Goebbels formed a secret unit within his ministry to leak fictitious stories about the alleged fortress to the West. These reports, which were accepted as true by U.S. and French intelligence officers and Supreme Allied Commander General Dwight D. Eisenhower himself, alluded to massive supplies of arms and food cached in impregnable bombproof caves, underground munitions factories, and special elite SS troops steeled to repel Allied attempts to occupy southern Germany.

With Hitler's sanction Goebbels was attempting to confuse top Allied leaders with these false reports. He succeeded admirably, much to the consternation of German army officers desperately driving their forces west in a determined effort to surrender to the Americans and British and avoid capture by the Soviets. Eisenhower fell victim to Goebbels's deception, turning away from Berlin and toward the south, to attack the fictitious fortress area. Berlin and Prague were left to the Soviets to overrun and occupy.

The Werewolves were another twist of Nazi propaganda aimed at creating even more difficulties for those Germans who survived the war. This was an alleged plan uniting the cream of the SS and the Hitler Youth into a strike force that would train in the mountains of southern Germany. From there they would conduct guerrilla warfare against the occupying Allies, much as the resistance movements did in the territories once occupied by the Germans.

Actually no mass guerrilla movement existed. The few Werewolves who were mobilized expected to fight behind enemy lines in full uniform, so that if they were captured, they would be accorded the rights of prisoners of war. As the fate of Nazi Germany became apparent, Goebbels aired radio talks over "Radio Werewolf." He described how these underground fighters, disguised as civilians, would attack

Allied occupation troops, killing individual soldiers, ambushing convoys, and blowing up military facilities. Since capture could subject them to execution, most of the Werewolves deserted and surrendered.

The Werewolves never existed as a viable combat force. They were a fabrication created by the moribund Nazi legion to incite Allied soldiers against the civilian population. The Nazis hoped this would result in the German people being treated the way the people of other nations were treated by their German occupiers.

Up to the final hour, fanatic Nazis were resolved to obey Hitler's maniacal dictum that if they could not conquer the world, "we should drag half the world into destruction with us."[7]

11

PROFILE OF A BUNGLER

> Amateurishness was one of
> Hitler's dominant traits.
>
> Albert Speer

Looking back from the vantage point of five decades and
with full knowledge of how the war ended, it is easy to indict
a defeated leader such as Adolf Hitler for committing many
grave blunders and miscalculations in his conduct of the war.
However, much the same could be said of Allied leaders, especially Winston Churchill and Dwight Eisenhower.

Of the former, Geoffrey Regan has written, "Like a latter-
day Chatham he scattered British forces, and lost many of
them, on ill-advised operations which detracted from the
central military aim."[1] As for Eisenhower, his efficient leadership of a diverse and frequently squabbling alliance of national armies will forever be stained by his decision to turn
away from the certain capture of Berlin. Instead he attacked
south, toward the "national redoubt," a fabrication of Nazi
propaganda and erroneous intelligence reports.

Hitler was an absolute dictator whose decisions were not easily challenged by his generals, men with greater military experience. Because of that, his mistakes were magnified much more than those of his enemies from democratic political systems, where more than one voice was heard on important military planning and operational matters. Hitler's unshakable belief in his own infallibility left no room for opposing views.

Several of Hitler's blunders had such far-reaching effects on the war that they cannot be tied to individual battles or campaigns. In a study of the dictator's life Robert G. L. Waite wrote that "Hitler's blunders were so many, so costly, and so gratuitous as to suggest that these 'mistakes' were the result of a strong, unconscious impulse for self-destruction."[2]

Among the worst of these far-reaching mistakes was Hitler's choice of friends, particularly Hermann Göring and Benito Mussolini. Hermann Göring achieved modest recognition during World War I as a fighter pilot who commanded the Richthofen Fighter Squadron after the death of the famous Red Baron. Hitler entrusted Göring with complete control of the Luftwaffe because he was a devoted Nazi and a loyal follower of the Führer, not because of his abilities as a commander. Göring performed satisfactorily while creating the German air force, but he failed miserably as its commander.

While Hitler was apt to ridicule Göring in private, it was not until a few days before his own death that the Führer lost faith in him. Göring had promised Hitler that his air force would annihilate the British troops on the beaches at Dunkirk. The German failure to prevent the British escape from Dunkirk rests almost as much with Göring as it does with Hitler. Instead of reprimanding Göring for his failure, Hitler promoted him to the exhalted rank of *Reichs marschall*. Göring failed once again to make good on a commitment to Hitler when he promised to drive the RAF from the skies over Britain. Again Hitler chose to ignore Göring's failure.

In November 1942 the German Sixth Army under General

von Paulus was surrounded at Stalingrad. It was obvious that the only hope of survival for the 300,000 troops trapped in the Soviet city was to be supplied by air. The Sixth Army required 30 tons of ammunition, 300 tons of fuel, and 150 tons of food every day. Hitler turned to Göring for help. Göring was spending little time commanding the Luftwaffe as he engaged in his favorite pastime of stealing art treasures from conquered nations. When Hitler called Göring and asked if the supplies could be flown into Stalingrad on a daily basis, Göring, ill-informed as usual concerning the current status and operational strength of the Luftwaffe, responded that it could be done.

Colonel-General von Richthofen, commanding the Fourth Air Force which would have to operate this airlift, noted that Paulus believed such an operation feasible, but he told his superiors he could not share this view. Had either Göring or [Air Staff Chief General Hans] Jeschonnek firmly challenged the proposal, Hitler would certainly have abandoned it and ordered Paulus to fight his way out of the encircling ring; but the proposal passed unchallenged at this stage.[3]

Even a casual glance at the inventory of operational transport planes available to the Luftwaffe at that time would clearly have shown that the task to which Göring had agreed was well outside the air force's capability.

In his history of the Luftwaffe, David Irving estimated it would require 800 Junker 52 transports to supply the beleaguered troops at Stalingrad. The entire Luftwaffe inventory was only 750 Ju 52s, of which several hundred were in Africa, flying supplies for the Afrika Corps. Desperately needed bombers, already in short supply, would have to be converted into transports to meet the needs of von Paulus's army.

Once again Hitler made a vital decision that became a major factor contributing to Germany's defeat. Based on

Göring's assurances, Hitler ordered the Sixth Army to remain in Stalingrad, where it was decimated, partly because it could not be supplied properly. The Soviets gained an enormous psychological and military advantage when they captured the German Sixth Army and altered the course of the war.

Hitler's reaction to Göring's repeated malfeasance was typical of his personal loyalty to Göring: "He is my own designated successor, and that is why I cannot hold him publicly responsible for Stalingrad."[4]

Italian dictator Benito Mussolini was another friend who cost Hitler dearly. When Mussolini gave Hitler his approval to take over Austria in 1938, the Nazi leader pledged undying friendship to the Italian. Before long, however, Hitler, the junior partner, amassed the greater army and assumed the greater role in the fascist relationship. Stung by his demotion, Mussolini embarked on military adventures well beyond the capabilities of his armed forces. German troops always needed to be ready to rescue the Italians.

An example of Mussolini's infantile attitude and ineptitude was his invasion of Greece on October 28, 1940. Despite his claims that the invasion had been planned well in advance, history records it as a simple case of attempted one-upmanship. The Italian was offended when he learned of the German occupation of Romania on October 7. He had met with Hitler three days earlier, but Hitler had made no mention of his plans to invade Romania. Mussolini was insulted by this snub and plotted a way to get even. He decided on an invasion of Greece. It was done with no advance notice to the Germans. In fact, Hitler learned about it while on the way to Florence to meet with Mussolini.

Hitler was furious when he received a telegram announcing the invasion of Greece had begun two hours earlier. He called it "madness. If he wanted to pick a fight with poor little Greece why didn't he attack in Malta or Crete? It would at least make some sense in the context of the war with Britain in the Mediterranean."[5] Mussolini made it clear to his foreign minister, Count Galeazzo Ciano, what was at the root of this foolhardy invasion: "Hitler always faces me with a fait accompli! This time I am going to pay him back in his own coin. He will find out in the papers that I have occupied Greece. In this way the equilibrium will be re-established."[6]

The invasion was a disaster for the Italians. The Italian army was totally unprepared, having demobilized and sent home some 300,000 soldiers only a few weeks earlier. Despite strong objections from his generals, Mussolini insisted on sending the 4 available combat divisions into Greece against that nation's 15 divisions. More than 20,000 Italian troops died fighting the Greeks, another 40,000 were wounded, and 26,000 were taken prisoner.

Within weeks the invasion faltered and stopped. The Greeks counterattacked and drove the main remnant of the Italian force into Albania and trapped others around several ports. Mussolini was forced to ask for Hitler's help—and the timing could not have been worse for Hitler. Most of his army was massed along Germany's eastern frontier, prepared to invade the Soviet Union. Hitler felt obligated to rescue his ally, so the Soviet invasion was delayed and nearly 700,000 German troops proceeded south to conquer Greece and Yugoslavia.

The alliance between Germany and Italy was a burden Hitler should have been smart enough to avoid. In 1941 Rommel was sent to North Africa to rescue Italian troops trapped by British Empire forces less than a quarter their strength. Hitler and Germany paid dearly for Mussolini's approval of the Nazi occupation of Austria. Whatever reason Hitler had for continuing the alliance, it was a serious mistake.

A fatal flaw in Hitler's leadership style was his practice of fragmenting responsibilities. One area in which this had a truly devastating effect was the development of technologically advanced weapons. It also affected every government activity, especially the conduct of the war. The major result of this lack of coordination was an absence of cooperation among Hitler's subordinates and between almost all government agencies. Every position of authority was duplicated, sometimes even triplicated. This system allowed Hitler to distribute many more important plums than his government would ordinarily need, but it also created rivalries among subordinates which ensured that if someone in high position spoke against Hitler or one of his policies, there would always be a rival to expose him.

This policy of pitting key people against one another worked to the detriment of a nation at war. The development of the atomic bomb is an example of the need for a unified effort. Every department of the U.S. government that might be involved in research and development of such a weapon, as well as the governments of Great Britain and Canada, worked together under one leader to accomplish their goal. Had there been an attempt to build an atomic bomb in Nazi Germany, the SS might have been working on one project, the Ministry of Armament working separately on another, and countless other departments working on their own. With the degree of competition and lack of cooperation exhibited by these segments of the Nazi government, there can be no question that the result would have been a waste of limited resources and manpower, and no bomb would have been built.

This fragmentation and duplication also ensured that many important projects would never succeed, especially when German resources shrank drastically and various departments were squabbling over what was available. As with the "miracle weapons," there were too many projects from too many agencies competing for too few materials. In the end, no one succeeded.

A decidedly dangerous outgrowth of this fragmentation was that Heinrich Himmler, through his SS organization, was able to take control of much of what went on inside the

Reich and the territories it occupied. The SS became a state within the German state. It had its own police force, the dreaded Gestapo; its own intelligence services, both at home and abroad; its own army, which reached a strength of 39 divisions; its own industrial empire, built on the backs of slave laborers taken from concentration and POW camps; and its own leader, Heinrich Himmler.

The result was that in virtually every endeavor the SS undermined the normal functions of the state. Because of Himmler's ruthlessness and his willingness to use every crime imaginable to further his goals, the SS succeeded in syphoning money away from war industries, research programs, and even the army. Wehrmacht generals constantly complained that the SS, never as well trained or led as the army, invariably received the best weapons available, leaving the remainder for the regular troops.

In the summer of 1944 Himmler told Speer that Hitler agreed with his efforts to make the SS a fully self-sufficient organization that did not rely on the German government or the head of state for its funding. Himmler complained that the SS was dependent on the minister of finances to meet its operating expenses. This did not matter, said Himmler, so long as the Führer was alive. However, the Führer agreed with him that it would be expedient to make the SS independent of the national budget on a long-term basis by having it construct its own factories as a financial foundation."[7]

Hitler regarded the SS as a powerful defense against his internal opponents, and a viable alternative to the traditional state agencies. The SS was loyal to Hitler personally, not to Germany. Yet, paradoxically, interference by the corrupt and mediocre SS leadership in the armaments industry created costly delays in the development of new weapons that easily could have altered the result of the war.

The SS leaders were drawn from a select few who showed early and absolute devotion to the Nazi Party. They were predominantly sycophants with little leadership ability or

capacity for innovative thought. Despite earning an unde-
served reputation for "typical German efficiency," the SS was
a burden on the German economy, industrial might, arms
development, and virtually everything in which Himmler involved it.

In the end the SS devoured itself when it treated the slave
laborers on whom its economy depended with cruel disregard. Had Hitler limited the SS to its original role of body-
guard troops or curtailed Himmler's insane opportunism,
Germany's economic and industrial strength would not have
been dissipated, and the development of advanced weapons
might have succeeded in altering the course of the war.[8]

Hitler's rabid anti-Semitism looms large as another under-
lying reason he lost the war. Yet it was as easily temporarily
discarded as that other basic precept of the Nazis, anti-
Bolshevism. It would have been possible for Hitler to cease
the persecution of Germany's Jews without serious opposition from his followers as easily as he disregarded anticom-
munism when he signed a pact with the Bolshevik devil
himself, Joseph Stalin.

Had Hitler deferred his persecution of the Jews at least
until he had consolidated the territory he planned to conquer
for the Greater Germany, the outcome of the war might have
been different. The potential contribution of Jewish scientists
and technicians to the German war effort was considerable.
The opportunity to do this came on June 30, 1934, when
Hitler and the SS murdered the leaders of the SA, the storm
troopers. The public associated the SA with the atrocities visited on the German Jews. If Hitler had set his priorities
clearly, he would have blamed the dead SA leaders for the attacks on Jews and put anti-Semitism on a back burner until
he accomplished his greater goals. This was precisely what
he did when he signed the pact with Stalin. His anti-
Bolshevism was temporarily subordinated so he could concentrate his military thrust to the west and not worry about
his eastern frontiers.

Historian Edwin Hoyt writes that "The showing of the Jews in Germany's past wars had always been excellent. There is no reason to believe that the Jews would have deserted Hitler or Germany had they not been persecuted. There is every reason to believe they would have accepted the trampling on general civil liberties as almost all other Germans did."[9]

Ronald Lewin believed that many German Jews had become "as much German as Jewish," and therefore were loyal German citizens. In Lewin's opinion, the persecution of the Jews cost Hitler dearly.

There is, indeed, nothing in principle to suggest that, had Hitler seen the value of somehow keeping the Jews "within the family" and led them into a "national" war, they would have rallied as they did in 1914. The results would have been incalculable. Hitler's self-imposed loss in the fields of science and technology was certainly substantial. But there is a more mundane point. As Russia took its toll, and the fighting fronts spread around the continent, Germany's shortage of manpower became increasingly critical. Hitler had sent to their death thousands and thousands of men who would have readily marched thither for the sake of Germany.[10]

As we have seen, Hitler's qualifications as a military leader left much to be desired. He was an amateur who conducted the largest war in history on the basis of his intuition. Because he lacked real training as either a leader or a military strategist or tactician, Hitler developed certain military dicta that ran counter to everything his military planners and officers tried to teach him. The most costly of these, especially in terms of the loss of troops, was his refusal to withdraw from a military objective once it was occupied.

It was a policy of fanatical resistance. On October 14, 1942, Hitler issued this order to his troops: "Every leader, down to squad leader must be convinced of his sacred duty to stand fast come what may even if the enemy outflanks him on the right and left, even if his part of the line is cut off, encircled, overrun by tanks, enveloped in smoke or gassed."[11]

Tactical retreat and strategic withdrawal were military maneuvers Hitler never understood. He liked telling his generals that when a German soldier walked on a piece of ground, that ground must never be surrendered to the enemy. It sounded very nice, but it simply was not reality. There are situations in war when a well-planned and orderly retreat from an indefensible position to one more easily defended is the correct action. This was beyond Hitler's comprehension.

In December 1941, with German forces bogged down in the frozen countryside of the Soviet Union and German generals seeking to withdraw to positions they could more readily defend against the growing Soviet army and in which their lightly clad troops had a better chance of surviving the weather, Hitler dealt a fatal blow to the German army.

Hitler dismissed several of his most able field commanders, including Field Marshal von Rundstedt and panzer generals Guderian and Erich Hoeppner, because they either advocated withdrawal or had withdrawn from previous positions against his orders. Pleading poor health, field marshals von Bock and von Leeb asked to be relieved. By the end of 1941 the commanders of all three invading army groups were gone. Hitler's direct control over their actions left the field marshals little room to act as effective field commanders. His policy of fanatical resistance, fighting to the death instead of prudent strategic withdrawal, drove Hitler's most experienced and knowledgeable general officers from the battlefield.

The most stunning example of the cost of Hitler's policy of no retreat came a year later at Stalingrad. German losses in that Soviet city were termed the "hinge of fate" by Winston Churchill. It was the turning point in the war, and it was turned against the Germans because Hitler, regardless of the reasons he cited, including Göring's inability to supply the trapped army by air, refused to permit the Sixth Army to withdraw from the city and fight the surrounding Soviet forces from a stronger position, one that could be reinforced by help from other German units. Field Marshal von Manstein, who attempted unsuccessfully to relieve the trapped Sixth Army, assessed the blame for the loss of several hundred thousand German and ally soldiers squarely on Hitler: "The cause of Sixth Army's destruction at Stalingrad is obviously to be found in Hitler's refusal—doubtless mainly for reasons of prestige—to give up the city voluntarily."[12]

Hitler had no regard for the lives of German soldiers. It was, as von Manstein said, a matter of prestige that Germans facing the choice of death or surrender should choose death. Apparently Hitler never considered that they would be lost forever to the future of Germany. An examination of the final communications between the beleaguered Sixth Army in Stalingrad and Hitler reveals the extent of the cruel disregard Hitler held for his own troops.

On January 8, 1943, three Soviet officers delivered to General von Paulus a message from their commander, General Konstantin Rokossovski. The Soviet general outlined the appalling condition of the German army trapped in Stalingrad and called for von Paulus to surrender. In return he offered rations for all German soldiers and medical treatment for the tens of thousands of wounded, and would permit all German prisoners to retain their badges of rank, their military decorations, and their personal belongings. Von Paulus radioed the full text of the message to Berlin, asking Hitler to give him freedom of action as he saw fit. Hitler refused.

Six days later the Soviets made another offer. Despite the urging of other German generals, some of whom, like von Manstein, were not in Stalingrad, to ignore Hitler and surrender, the obedient von Paulus begged Hitler to allow him to surrender.

Troops without ammunition or food. . . . Effective command no longer possible . . . 18,000 wounded without any supplies or dressings or drugs. . . . Further defense senseless. Collapse inevitable.

Army requests immediate permission to surrender in order to save
lives of remaining troops.[13]

Hitler radioed back that surrender was forbidden and that
the Sixth Army was to hold its positions to the last man. On
January 31, 1943, the radio operator at Sixth Army headquarters signed off with a final message that the Soviets were
at the door of their bunker and all remaining equipment was
being destroyed. More than 90,000 German soldiers were
taken prisoner at Stalingrad. Over 85,000 died in captivity.

Hundreds of thousands of German soldiers, and others
fighting alongside them, lost their lives in Africa, western
Europe, Italy, the Soviet Union, and, in the final weeks, in
Germany itself because Hitler refused to allow them to withdraw from untenable positions. This massive loss of manpower and armaments crippled the German army irrepara-
bly. Hoyt described Hitler's attitude correctly: "Their Führer
cared nothing for his soldiers' lives or welfare. 'Hold the line'
was his watchword. Hold the line no matter the cost, no matter whether it was worth holding or what holding it would
mean for the future."[14]

In spite of Hitler's preoccupation with the development of
new weapons, he possessed one major weapon that he never
truly understood, and misused throughout the war. This was
the U-boat. The German U-boats of World War II have received so much publicity that we are left with the impression
that Hitler employed these warships with deadly effect. This
was far from true.

The value of the underwater warships as predators of merchant shipping was lost on Hitler. Impressed by the questionable success of U-47 when it penetrated the defenses around
Scapa Flow, north of Scotland, on October 14, 1939, and
sank the British battleship *Royal Oak*, Hitler insisted the
U-boats concentrate on British warships, an arena where
they were largely outgunned and outnumbered.

In January 1939 Hitler was presented with two options for

a building program for the German navy. One concentrated on building surface vessels, and the other placed increased emphasis on expanding the U-boat fleet. He chose the construction of surface ships, including what he called superbattleships. Admiral Karl Doenitz, Germany's famed commander of the U-boats, requested a contingent of at least 300 vessels. At the start of the war he had less than one-quarter that number. Not until late in the war were U-boats capable of running underwater for extended periods approved by Hitler. Again, it was too late to make a difference in the war's outcome.

Adolf Hitler failed as a military commander because he was not suited for the job. Although he was an excellent motivator of the masses and an inspired speaker, he never understood that personal willpower could not overcome poorly trained or equipped troops, lack of modern weapons, or lack of thorough planning. He was an amateur whose bungling and reckless venture into war caused the deaths of millions of people.

We will never know exactly what would have happened if Hitler had been stopped by the French and British when he made his first weak, tentative moves toward expansion. Some historians believe that had he been forced to abandon his plans for conquest before blood was shed, at any time between his march into the Rhineland and his invasion of Poland, Adolf Hitler would be remembered today as a great leader. Perhaps so, but there is no escaping the fact that Hitler was not a rational man. His belief in his personal superiority and his disregard for human life were always present. No leader can rule a nation using his willpower and intuition as the basis of decisions and be considered a great leader.

Hitler's intuition, on which he based many military decisions, was no substitute for solid ability based on experience. Field Marshal von Manstein sums up:

While Hitler may have had an eye for tactical opportunity and could quickly seize a chance when it was offered to him, he still lacked the ability to assess the prerequisites and practicability of a plan of operations. He failed to understand that the objectives and ultimate scope of an operation must be in direct proportion to the time and forces needed to carry it out—to say nothing of the possibilities of supply. He did not—or would not—realize that any long-range offensive operation calls for a steady build-up of troops over and above those committed in the original assault.[15]

NOTES

Introduction

1. Ronald Lewin, *Hitler's Mistakes* (New York: Morrow, 1984), 101.

2. David Irving, *The War Path: Hitler's Germany 1933–1939* (New York: Viking, 1978), 48.

3. Erich von Manstein, *Lost Victories,* edited and translated by Anthony G. Powell (Chicago: Regnery, 1958), 276.

4. Percy Ernst Schramm, *Hitler: The Man and the Military Leader,* translated by Donald S. Detwiler (Chicago: Quadrangle, 1971), 110.

5. Adolf Hitler, *Secret Conversations,* translated by Norman Cameron and R. H. Stevens (New York: Signet, 1953), 259.

6. Schramm, *Hitler,* 111.

7. Albert Speer, *Inside The Third Reich,* translated by Richard Winston and Clara Winston (New York: Collier, 1981), 198.

Chapter 1

1. William L. Shirer, *The Rise and Fall of The Third Reich* (New York: Simon and Schuster, 1960), 31.

2. Albert Speer, *Inside The Third Reich*, translated by Richard Winston and Clara Winston (New York: Collier, 1981), 72.

3. Dr. Earl Ziemke, interview for the film *How Hitler Lost the War* (Varied Directions, 1989).

4. David Irving, *The War Path: Hitler's Germany 1933–1939* (New York: Viking, 1978), 86.

5. Peter Hoffmann, *The History of the German Resistance, 1933–1945*, translated by Richard Barry (Cambridge: MIT, 1977), 49–96.

6. B. H. Liddell Hart, *History of the Second World War* (New York: Putnam's, 1970), 10.

7. Winston Churchill, *Memoirs of the Second World War* (New York: Bonanza, 1978), 147.

8. Winston Churchill, *The Gathering Storm* (Boston: Houghton Mifflin, 1948), 311–12.

9. Irving, *The War Path*, 265.

10. Erich von Manstein, *Lost Victories*, edited and translated by Anthony G. Powell (Chicago: Regnery, 1958), 62.

11. David Irving, *The Rise and Fall of the Luftwaffe: The Life of Field Marshal Erhard Milch* (Boston: Little, Brown, 1973), 83.

12. William L. Shirer, *The Collapse of the Third Republic* (New York: Simon and Schuster, 1969), 522.

13. Walter Warlimont, *Inside Hitler's Headquarters 1939–1945*, translated by R. H. Barry (New York: Praeger, 1964), 205–6.

14. Von Manstein, *Lost Victories*, 71.

15. Robert Payne, *The Life and Death of Adolf Hitler* (New York: Praeger, 1973), 286.

Chapter 2

1. Robert Payne, *The Life and Death of Adolf Hitler* (New York: Praeger, 1973), 383.

2. B. H. Liddell Hart, *History of the Second World War* (New York: Putnam's, 1970), 81.

3. Jeffrey Page, interview for the film *How Hitler Lost the War* (Varied Directions, 1989).

4. B. H. Liddell Hart, *The German Generals Talk* (New York: Morrow/Quill, 1979), 133.

5. John Toland, *Adolf Hitler* (Garden City, NY: Doubleday, 1976), 839.

6. Erich von Manstein, *Lost Victories*, edited and translated by Anthony G. Powell (Chicago: Regnery, 1958), 74.

7. Liddell Hart, *German Generals*, 133.

8. Von Manstein, *Lost Victories*, 124.

9. Kenneth Macksey, *Military Errors of World War Two* (London: Arms & Armour, 1987), 37.

10. Edwin P. Hoyt, *Hitler's War* (New York: McGraw-Hill, 1988), 145.

11. Richard Brett-Smith, *Hitler's Generals* (San Rafael, CA: Presidio, 1977), 23.

12. Wilhelm Keitel, *The Memoirs of Field Marshal Keitel*, edited by William Goerlitz, translated by David Irving, (New York: Stein & Day, 1965), 114.

13. Liddell Hart, *History*, 82.

14. Brett-Smith, *Hitler's Generals*, 279.

15. Liddell Hart, *History*, 83.

16. Ibid.

17. Payne, *Life and Death*, 384.

18. Toland, *Adolf Hitler*, 833.

19. Liddell Hart, *History*, 81.

20. Allen Andrews, *The Air Marshals* (New York: Morrow, 1970), 80.

21. Nicholas Harman, *Dunkirk: The Patriotic Myth* (New York: Simon and Schuster, 1980), 30.

22. David Irving, *Hitler's War* (New York: Avon, 1990), 290.

23. Brett-Smith, *Hitler's Generals*, 110.

24. Liddell Hart, *German Generals*, 134.

25. William L. Shirer, *The Rise and Fall of the Third Reich* (New York: Simon and Schuster, 1960), 734.

26. Payne, *Life and Death*, 385.

27. Brett-Smith, *Hitler's Generals*, 22.

28. Shirer, *Third Reich*, 737.

29. Hoyt, *Hitler's War*, 145.

30. Liddell Hart, *History*, 74.

31. William L. Shirer, *The Collapse of The Third Republic* (New York: Simon and Schuster, 1969), 26.

32. Guy Chapman, *Why France Fell* (New York: Holt, Rinehart and Winston, 1969), 334.

Chapter 3

1. William L. Shirer, *The Rise and Fall of the Third Reich* (New York: Simon and Schuster, 1960), 486.
2. Robert Payne, *The Life and Death of Adolf Hitler* (New York: Praeger, 1973), 370.
3. Adolf Hitler, *Blitzkrieg to Defeat: Hitler's War Directives 1939–1945*, edited by H. R. Trevor-Roper (New York: Holt, Rinehart and Winston, 1965), 34–37.
4. Payne, *Life and Death*, 416.
5. David Irving, *The Rise and Fall of the Luftwaffe* (Boston: Little, Brown, 1973), 91.
6. Ibid.
7. Ibid.
8. Irving, *Rise and Fall*, 92.
9. B. H. Liddell Hart, *History of the Second World War* (New York: Putnam's, 1970), 708.
10. Ronald Lewin, *Hitler's Mistakes* (New York: Morrow, 1986), 109.
11. Sir Christopher Foxley Norris, interview for the film *How Hitler Lost the War* (Varied Directions, 1989).
12. Winston S. Churchill, *Memoirs of the Second World War* (New York: Bonanza, 1978), 284–85.
13. Irving, *Rise and Fall*, 94.
14. Payne, *Life and Death*, 394.
15. David Irving, *Hitler's War* (New York: Avon, 1990), 294.
16. Peter Fleming, *Operation Sea Lion* (New York: Simon and Schuster, 1957), 39.
17. Irving, *Hitler's War*, 298.
18. Shirer, *Third Reich*, 752.
19. Ibid., 751.
20. Hitler, *Blitzkrieg to Defeat*, 36.
21. Norman Rich, *Hitler's War Aims* (New York: Norton, 1974), 395.

22. David Irving, *Göring: A Biography* (New York: Morrow, 1989), 292.

23. Telford Taylor, *The Breaking Wave* (New York: Simon and Schuster, 1967), 204.

24. Richard Collier, *1940: The Avalanche* (New York: Dial/James Wade, 1979), 196.

25. Cajus Bekker, *Hitler's Naval War* (New York: Zebra, 1981), 169.

26. Fleming, *Operation Sea Lion,* 298.

Chapter 4

1. Edwin P. Hoyt, *Hitler's War* (New York: McGraw-Hill, 1988), 162.

2. Seymour Freidin and William Richardson, eds., *The Fatal Decisions* (New York: Sloane, 1956), 19.

3. David Irving, *Hitler's War* (New York: Avon, 1990), 309.

4. Martin Gilbert, *The Second World War* (New York: Holt, 1989), 117.

5. Richard Collier, *1940: The Avalanche* (New York: Dial/James Wade, 1979), 188.

6. Gilbert, *Second World War,* 118.

7. Collier, *1940,* 190.

8. Hoyt, *Hitler's War,* 164.

9. Samuel W. Mitcham, Jr., *Men of the Luftwaffe* (Novato, CA: Presidio, 1988), 103.

10. Robert Payne, *The Life and Death of Adolf Hitler* (New York: Praeger, 1973), 403.

11. David Irving, *Göring: A Biography* (New York: Morrow, 1989), 296.

12. Hoyt, *Hitler's War,* 166.

13. Allen Andrews, *The Air Marshals* (New York: Morrow, 1970), 131.

14. Winston S. Churchill, *Their Finest Hour* (Boston: Houghton Mifflin, 1949), 331.

Chapter 5

1. Winston S. Churchill, *Memoirs of the Second World War* (New York: Bonanza, 1978), 469.

2. Ronald Lewin, *Hitler's Mistakes* (New York: Morrow, 1986), 117.

3. B. H. Liddell Hart, *History of the Second World War* (New York: Putnam's, 1970), 158.

4. Richard Brett-Smith, *Hitler's Generals* (San Rafael, CA: Presidio, 1977), 27.

5. Lewin, *Mistakes*, 120.

6. Seymour Freidin and William Richardson, eds., *The Fatal Decisions* (New York: Sloane, 1956), 66.

7. Lewin, *Mistakes*, 117.

8. Ibid., 118.

9. Ibid.

10. Dr. Earl Ziemke, interview for the film *How Hitler Lost the War* (Varied Directions, 1989).

11. Bryan I. Fugate, *Operation Barbarossa* (Novato, CA: Presidio, 1984), 80.

12. Lewin, *Mistakes*, 119.

13. B. H. Liddell Hart, *The Other Side of the Hill* (London: Cassell, 1951), 251.

14. Liddell Hart, *History*, 131.

15. Earl F. Ziemke and Magna E. Bauer, *Moscow to Stalingrad: Decision in the East* (New York: Military Heritage, 1988), 33.

16. Alfred W. Turney, *Disaster at Moscow: Von Bock's Campaigns, 1941-1942* (Albuquerque: University of New Mexico, 1970), 74.

17. Ibid., 82.

18. Joseph Goebbels, *The Goebbels Diaries 1942-1943*, edited and translated by Louis P. Lochner (Garden City, NY: Doubleday, 1948), 135.

19. Robert Payne, *The Life and Death of Adolf Hitler* (New York: Praeger, 1973), 444.

20. Erich von Manstein, *Lost Victories*, edited and translated by Anthony G. Powell (Chicago: Regnery, 1958), 365.

Chapter 6

1. Robert Conquest, *The Harvest of Sorrow* (New York: Oxford University, 1984), 306.
2. Robert C. Tucker, ed., *Stalinism* (New York: Norton, 1977), 212.
3. Ronald Lewin, *Hitler's Mistakes* (New York: Morrow, 1984), 127.
4. Martin Gilbert, *The Second World War* (New York: Holt, 1989), 213.
5. Robert Leckie, *Delivered from Evil* (New York: Harper & Row, 1987), 288.
6. Peter J. Huxley-Blythe, *The East Came West* (Caldwell, ID: Caxton, 1964), 19.
7. Roland Gaucher, *Opposition in the USSR, 1917–1967*, translated by Charles Lam Markman (New York: Funk & Wagnalls, 1969), 292.
8. Erich von Manstein, *Lost Victories*, edited and translated by Anthony G. Powell (Chicago: Regnery, 1958), 175–76.
9. Mark R. Elliott, *Pawns of Yalta: Soviet Refugees and America's Role in Their Repatriation* (Champaign: University of Illinois, 1988), 16.
10. Gaucher, *Opposition*, 303.
11. J. F. C. Fuller, *Decisive Battles of the Western World*, Vol. III (New York: Funk & Wagnalls, 1956), 434.
12. Matthew Cooper, *The Nazi War Against Soviet Partisans 1941–1945* (Briarcliff Manor, NY: Stein & Day, 1979), 20.

Chapter 7

1. Robert G. L. Waite, *The Psychopathic God Adolf Hitler* (New York: Basic Books, 1977), 490, 497.
2. John Toland, *Adolf Hitler* (Garden City, NY: Doubleday, 1976), 959.
3. Waite, *Psychopathic God*, 490.
4. Wayne S. Cole, *Charles A. Lindbergh and the Battle Against American Intervention in World War II* (New York: Harcourt Brace Jovanovich, 1970), 8.
5. David Irving, *Hitler's War* (New York: Avon, 1990), 332.

6. William L. Shirer, *The Rise and Fall of the Third Reich* (New York: Simon and Schuster, 1960), 890.

7. Toland, *Adolf Hitler*, 951.

8. Ibid., 952.

9. Shirer, *Third Reich*, 894.

10. Ibid., 898.

11. Wilhelm Keitel, *The Memoirs of Field Marshal Wilhelm Keitel*, edited by Walter Goerlitz, translated by David Irving (New York: Stein & Day, 1965), 162.

12. Adolf Hitler, *Blitzkrieg to Defeat: Hitler's War Directives 1939–1945*, edited by H. R. Trevor-Roper (New York: Holt, Rinehart and Winston, 1965), 107.

13. Toland, *Adolf Hitler*, 953.

Chapter 8

1. Seymour Freidin and William Richardson, eds., *The Fatal Decisions* (New York: Sloane, 1956), 203.

2. Friedrich Ruge, *Rommel in Normandy* (San Rafael, CA: Presidio, 1979), 43.

3. Samuel W. Mitcham, Jr., *Rommel's Last Battle* (Briarcliff Manor, NY: Stein & Day, 1983), 21.

4. Albert Speer, *Inside the Third Reich*, translated by Richard Winston and Clara Winston (New York: Collier, 1981), 352.

5. Freidin and Richardson, *Fatal Decisions*, 202.

6. Kenneth Macksey, *Military Errors of World War Two* (London: Arms & Armour, 1987), 180.

7. Gordon A. Harrison, *U.S. Army in World War II: The European Theater of Operations, Cross-Channel Attack* (Washington, DC: U.S. Government Printing Office, 1951), 258.

8. Freidin and Richardson, *Fatal Decisions*, 214.

9. Speer, *Third Reich*, 354.

10. John Keegan, *Six Armies in Normandy* (New York: Viking, 1982), 65.

11. Robert Payne, *The Life and Death of Adolf Hitler* (New York: Praeger, 1973), 496.

Chapter 9

1. Albert Speer, *Inside the Third Reich*, translated by Richard Winston and Clara Winston (New York: Collier, 1981), 227.

2. Ibid.

3. Walter Dornberger, *V-2*, translated by James Cleugh and Geoffrey Halliday (New York: Viking, 1958), 196.

4. Speer, *Third Reich*, 262.

5. David Irving, *The Rise and Fall of the Luftwaffe: The Life of Field Marshal Erhard Milch* (Boston: Little, Brown, 1973), 219, 251.

6. Speer, *Third Reich*, 363.

7. David Irving, *Göring: A Biography* (New York: Morrow, 1989), 414.

8. Speer, *Third Reich*, 364.

9. Ibid.

10. Ibid., 365.

11. Brian Ford, *German Secret Weapons: Blueprint for Mars* (New York: Ballantine, 1969), 159.

12. Ronald Lewin, *Hitler's Mistakes* (New York: Morrow, 1986), 93.

Chapter 10

1. Robert Payne, *The Life and Death of Adolf Hitler* (New York: Praeger, 1973), 498.

2. Richard Brett-Smith, *Hitler's Generals* (San Rafael, CA: Presidio, 1977), 35.

3. Albert Speer, *Inside the Third Reich*, translated by Richard Winston and Clara Winston (New York: Collier, 1981), 440.

4. Adolf Hitler, *Blitzkrieg to Defeat: Hitler's War Directives 1939–1945*, edited by H. R. Trevor-Roper (New York: Holt, Rinehart and Winston, 1965), 207.

5. Cornelius Ryan, *The Last Battle* (New York: Simon and Schuster, 1966), 83.

6. Rodney G. Minott, *The Fortress That Never Was* (New York: Holt, Rinehart and Winston, 1964), 25.

7. H. R. Trevor-Roper, *The Last Days of Hitler* (New York: Macmillan, 1947), 47.

Chapter 11

1. Geoffrey Regan, *Great Military Disasters* (New York: Evans, 1987), 115.

2. Robert G. L. Waite, *The Psychopathic God Adolf Hitler* (New York: Basic Books, 1977), 481.

3. David Irving, *The Rise and Fall of the Luftwaffe: The Life of Field Marshal Erhard Milch* (Boston: Little, Brown, 1973), 176.

4. Ibid., 197.

5. Richard Collier, *Duce! A Biography of Benito Mussolini* (New York: Viking, 1971), 178.

6. Ibid.

7. Albert Speer, *Infiltration*, translated by Joachim Neugroschel (New York: Macmillan, 1981), 174.

8. For a thorough investigation of the SS effect on arms production, see Speer, *Infiltration*.

9. Edwin P. Hoyt, *Hitler's War* (New York: McGraw-Hill, 1988), 34.

10. Ronald Lewin, *Hitler's Mistakes* (New York: Morrow, 1986), 46.

11. Earl F. Ziemke, *Stalingrad to Berlin: The German Defeat in the East* (New York: Military Heritage, 1985), 22.

12. Erich von Manstein, *Lost Victories*, edited and translated by Anthony G. Powell (Chicago: Regnery, 1958), 290.

13. Robert Payne, *The Life and Death of Adolf Hitler* (New York: Praeger, 1973), 930.

14. Hoyt, *Hitler's War*, 302.

15. Manstein, *Lost Victories*, 275.

SELECTED
BIBLIOGRAPHY

Adams, Henry H. *1942: The Year That Doomed the Axis*. New York: McKay, 1967.

Andrews, Allen. *The Air Marshals*. New York: Morrow, 1970.

Bailey, Thomas A., and Paul B. Ryan. *Hitler vs. Roosevelt: The Undeclared Naval War*. New York: Free Press, 1979.

Baldwin, Hanson W. *The Crucial Years 1939–1941: The World at War*. New York: Harper & Row, 1976.

Bartov, Omer. *The Eastern Front, 1941–45: German Troops and the Barbarisation of Warfare*. New York: St. Martin's, 1986.

Baudot, Marcel, ed. *The Historical Encyclopedia of World War II*. New York: Facts on File, 1980.

Bekker, Cajus. *Hitler's Naval War*. New York: Zebra, 1981.

Brett-Smith, Richard. *Hitler's Generals*. San Rafael, CA: Presidio, 1977.

Brever, William B. *Death of a Nazi Army: The Falaise Pocket*. Briarcliff Manor, NY: Stein & Day, 1985.

Calvocoressi, Peter, and Guy Wint. *Total War*. New York: Penguin, 1979.

Cecil, Robert. *Hitler's Decision to Invade Russia, 1941*. New York: McKay, 1975.

Chapman, Guy. *Why France Fell*. New York: Holt, Rinehart and Winston, 1969.

Chuikov, Vasili Ivanovich. *The Battle for Stalingrad*. Translated by Harold Silver. New York: Holt, Rinehart and Winston, 1964.

Churchill, Winston S. *The Gathering Storm*. Boston: Houghton Mifflin, 1948.

———. *Their Finest Hour*. Boston: Houghton Mifflin, 1949.

———. *Triumph and Tragedy*. Boston: Houghton Mifflin, 1953.

———. *Memoirs of the Second World War*. New York: Bonanza, 1978.

Cole, Wayne S. *Charles A. Lindbergh and the Battle Against American Intervention in World War II*. New York: Harcourt Brace Jovanovich, 1974.

Collier, Basil. *The Battle of the V-Weapons*. New York: Morrow, 1965.

Collier, Richard. *The City That Would Not Die*. New York: Dutton, 1960.

———. *EagleDay*. New York: Dutton, 1960.

———. *Duce! A Biography of Benito Mussolini*. New York: Viking, 1971.

———. *1940: The Avalanche*. New York: Dial/James Wade, 1979.

Conquest, Robert. *The Harvest of Sorrow*. New York: Oxford University, 1984.

Cooper, Matthew. *The Nazi War Against Soviet Partisans 1941–1945*. Briarcliff Manor, NY: Stein & Day, 1979.

Creveld, Martin van. *Hitler's Strategy 1940–1941: The Balkan Campaign*. London: Cambridge University, 1973.

Dollinger, Hans. *The Decline and Fall of Nazi Germany and Imperial Japan*. New York: Bonanza, 1967.

Dornberger, Walter. *V-2*. Translated by James Cleugh and Geoffrey Halliday. New York: Viking, 1958.

Downing, David. *The Devil's Virtuosos: German Generals at War, 1940–1945*. New York: St. Martin's, 1977.

Elliott, Mark R. *Pawns of Yalta: Soviet Refugees and America's Role in Their Repatriation*. Champaign: University of Illinois, 1981.

Fair, Charles. *From the Jaws of Victory*. New York: Simon and Schuster, 1971.

Fleming, Peter. *Operation Sea Lion*. New York: Simon and Schuster, 1957.

Ford, Brian. *German Secret Weapons: Blueprint for Mars*. New York: Ballantine, 1969.

Freidin, Seymour, and William Richardson, eds. *The Fatal Decisions*. New York: Sloane, 1956.

Friedlander, Saul. *Prelude to Downfall: Hitler and the United States, 1939–1941*. New York: Knopf, 1967.

Fugate, Bryan I. *Operation Barbarossa*. Novato, CA: Presidio, 1984.

Gaucher, Roland. *Opposition in the U.S.S.R. 1917–1967*. Translated by Charles Lam Markman. New York: Funk & Wagnalls, 1969.

Gavin, James M. *On to Berlin*. New York: Viking, 1978.

Gelb, Norman. *Scramble: A Narrative History of the Battle of Britain*. New York: Harcourt Brace Jovanovich, 1985.

Gilbert, Martin. *The Second World War: A Complete History*. New York: Holt, 1989.

Goebbels, Joseph. *The Goebbels Diaries 1942–1943*. Edited and translated by Louis P. Lochner. Garden City, NY: Doubleday, 1948.

Goldsmith-Carter, George. *The Battle of Britain: The Home Front*. New York: Lipscomb, 1974.

Harman, Nicholas. *Dunkirk: The Patriotic Myth*. New York: Simon and Schuster, 1980.

Higgins, Trumbull. *Hitler and Russia: The Third Reich in a Two Front War 1937–1943*. New York: Macmillan, 1966.

Hilderbrand, Klaus. *The Foreign Policy of the Third Reich*. Translated by Anthony Fothergill. Berkeley: University of California, 1979.

_____. *The Third Reich*. Translated by P. S. Falla. London: George Allen & Unwin, 1984.

Hitler, Adolf. *Blitzkrieg to Defeat: Hitler's War Directives 1939–1945*. Edited by H. R. Trevor-Roper. New York: Holt, Rinehart and Winston, 1965.

Hoffmann, Peter. *The History of the German Resistance, 1933–1945*. Translated by Richard Barry. Cambridge: MIT, 1977.

Hough, Richard, and Denis Richards. *The Battle of Britain: The Greatest Air Battle of World War II.* New York: Norton, 1989.

Hoyt, Edwin P. *Hitler's War.* New York: McGraw-Hill, 1988.

Huxley-Blythe, Peter J. *The East Came West.* Caldwell, ID: Caxton, 1964.

Irving, David. *The Rise and Fall of the Luftwaffe: The Life of Field Marshal Erhard Milch.* Boston: Little, Brown, 1973.

_____. *The War Path: Hitler's Germany 1933–1939.* New York: Viking, 1978.

_____. *Göring: A Biography.* New York: Morrow, 1989.

_____. *Hitler's War.* New York: Avon, 1990.

Keegan, John. *Six Armies in Normandy.* New York: Viking, 1982.

Keitel, Wilheim. *The Memoirs of Field Marshal Keitel.* Edited by Walter Goerlitz, translated by David Irving. New York: Stein & Day, 1965.

Kerr, Walter. *The Secret of Stalingrad.* Garden City, NY: Doubleday, 1978.

Langer, Walter C. *The Mind of Adolf Hitler.* New York: Basic Books, 1972.

Leach, Barry A. *German Strategy Against Russia 1939–1941.* London: Oxford University, 1973.

Leckie, Robert. *Delivered from Evil.* New York: Harper & Row, 1987.

Lee, Stephen J. *The European Dictatorships 1918–1945.* New York: Methuen, 1987.

Lewin, Ronald. *Hitler's Mistakes.* New York: Morrow, 1984.

Liddell Hart, B. H. *The Other Side of the Hill.* London: Cassell, 1951.

_____. *Strategy.* New York: Praeger, 1954.

_____. *History of the Second World War.* New York: Putnam's, 1970.

_____. *The German Generals Talk.* New York: Morrow/Quill, 1979.

Luck, Hans von. *Panzer Commander.* New York: Praeger, 1989.

Lukacs, John. *The Last European War, Sept. 1939–Dec. 1941.* Garden City, NY: Doubleday, 1976.

Macksey, Kenneth. *Military Errors of World War Two.* London: Arms & Armour, 1987.

Manstein, Erich von. *Lost Victories.* Edited and translated by Anthony G. Powell. Chicago: Regnery, 1958.

McKee, Alexander. *Strike from the Sky: The Story of the Battle of Britain*. Boston: Little, Brown, 1960.

Meskill, Johanna Menzel. *Hitler and Japan: The Hollow Alliance*. New York: Atherton, 1966.

Michel, Henri. *The Second World War*. Translated by Douglas Parmée. New York: Praeger, 1975.

Minott, Rodney G. *The Fortress That Never Was*. New York: Holt, Rinehart and Winston, 1964.

Mitcham, Samuel W., Jr. *Rommel's Last Battle: The Desert Fox and the Normandy Campaign*. Briarcliff Manor, NY: Stein & Day, 1983.

_____. *Men of the Luftwaffe*. Novato, CA: Presidio, 1988.

Parkinson, Roger. *Summer 1940: The Battle of Britain*. New York: McKay, 1977.

Payne, Robert. *The Life and Death of Adolf Hitler*. New York: Praeger, 1973.

Regan, Geoffrey. *Great Military Disasters*. New York: Evans, 1987.

Rich, Norman. *Hitler's War Aims: The Establishment of the New Order*. New York: Norton, 1974.

Rommel, Erwin. *The Rommel Papers*. Translated by B. H. Liddell Hart. New York: Harcourt, Brace, 1953.

Ruge, Friedrich. *Rommel in Normandy*. Translated by Ursula R. Moessner. San Rafael, CA: Presidio, 1979.

Ryan, Cornelius. *The Last Battle*. New York: Simon and Schuster, 1966.

Schram, Percy Ernst. *Hitler: The Man and the Military Leader*. Translated by Donald S. Detwiler. Chicago: Quadrangle, 1971.

Shirer, William L. *The Rise and Fall of the Third Reich: A History of Nazi Germany*. New York: Simon and Schuster, 1960.

_____. *The Collapse of the Third Republic*. New York: Simon and Schuster, 1969.

Shtemenko, S. M. *The Last Six Months*. Translated by Guy Daniels. Garden City, NY: Doubleday, 1977.

Snyder, Louis L. *Louis L. Snyder's Historical Guide to World War II*. Westport, CT: Greenwood, 1982.

Spears, Sir Edward. *Prelude to Dunkirk, July 1939–May 1940.* New York: Wyn, 1954.

Speer, Albert. *Inside The Third Reich.* Translated by Richard Winston and Clara Winston. New York: Collier, 1981.

———. *Infiltration.* Translated by Joachim Neugroschel. New York: Macmillan, 1981.

Steenberg, Sven. *Vlasov.* New York: Knopf, 1970.

Stephan, John J. *The Russian Fascists.* New York: Harper & Row, 1978.

Taylor, A. J. P. *The War Lords.* New York: Atheneum, 1978.

Taylor, Telford. *The Breaking Wave: World War II in the Summer of 1940.* New York: Simon and Schuster, 1967.

Toland, John. *Adolf Hitler.* Garden City, NY: Doubleday, 1976.

Topitsch, Ernst. *Stalin's War.* Translated by A. Taylor. New York: St. Martin's, 1988.

Trevor-Roper, H. R. *The Last Days of Hitler.* New York: Macmillan, 1947.

Tucker, Robert C., ed. *Stalinism.* New York: Norton, 1977.

Tunney, Christopher. *A Biographical Dictionary of World War II.* New York: St. Martin's, 1972.

Turney, Alfred W. *Disaster at Moscow: Von Bock's Campaigns 1941–1942.* Albuquerque: University of New Mexico, 1970.

Van Der Vat, Dan. *The Atlantic Campaign.* New York: Harper & Row, 1988.

Waite, Robert G. L. *The Psychopathic God Adolf Hitler.* New York: Basic Books, 1977.

Wilmont, Chester. *The Struggle for Europe.* New York: Harper & Bros., 1952.

Ziemke, Earl F. *Stalingrad to Berlin: The German Defeat in the East.* New York: Military Heritage, 1985.

Ziemke, Earl F., and Magna E. Bauer. *Moscow to Stalingrad: Decision in the East.* New York: Military Heritage, 1988.

INDEX

Copyright Acknowledgments

About the Author

JAMES P. DUFFY is a writer and lecturer. A life-long interest in military history, especially decisions that resulted in victory or defeat, led to this, his fourth book.